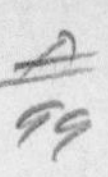

Dec, 1969

POEMS AND LETTERS OF NIKOLAUS LENAU

Translated, with an Introduction, by

WINTHROP H. ROOT

With German poems and English versions on facing pages

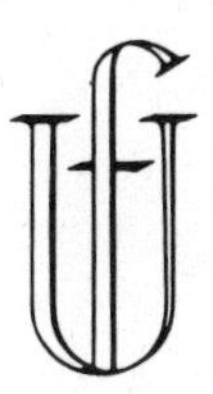

FREDERICK UNGAR PUBLISHING CO.
NEW YORK

Printed in the United States of America

Library of Congress Catalog Card No. 64-15296

To

W.M.E.

ACKNOWLEDGMENTS

The many colleagues and friends who have read and criticized these translations deserve a word of thanks for their encouragement and helpful suggestions. I cannot, unfortunately, name them all, but I wish to express here a special debt of gratitude to several of them whose perceptive and detailed criticisms have helped me improve the translations: Mrs. Wendell Triller; Professor Walter A. Reichart of the University of Michigan; Professor Emeritus E. Merrill Root of Earlham College; and my colleagues at Williams College, Professor William A. Little, Professor Emeritus Nelson S. Bushnell and Professor Harlan P. Hanson.

To my wife I am especially indebted for her encouragement, her repeated critical readings of the manuscript, and her willingness to put up with the poetic agonizings that seem, at least in this case, to be part of the labor of translating.

To Mrs. Sidney Ross who read proof I am sincerely grateful.

To Mr. William M. Emerson I owe a special debt of gratitude for his interest and encouragement.

W. H. R.

CONTENTS

NIKOLAUS LENAU

The searcher who would cross the far landscape of time into the past to bring back—a prose Orpheus seeking Eurydice in the shadows of the underworld—his vision of some long dead poet does well to tread warily and modestly. He catches glimpses of the remote figure he seeks, now shrouded in wind-blown mist, now in deep shadow and now in the bright sunlight. Gradually, as the heart and mind become accustomed to the sharply contrasting lights and shadows of the realm of history, the fragmentary glimpses are fused into a vision; a sudden light falls, at least for the searcher, upon the figure he has sought and he dares attempt to share his vision with others. The vision is made possible because in part the heart is involved, because love, a sense of kinship and sympathy, obtains between the searcher and the sought; if we have not love, we are, here as always—nothing. The emotional involvement need not be, indeed, it were better not to be, complete identification of the one self with the other; it is most creative as a profound awareness of the significance of the other's existence and the hidden springs of his motivation. But the heart alone is not enough, for emotional involvement can blind as well as open the eyes; the vision can become blurred when the heart beats too violently. There must also be the detachment we call objectivity; we must see as clearly as we feel; knowledge must exist beside emotion, clarity beside charity. Perhaps there is no better symbol of this than that the too involved Orpheus could not, for very love, bring back Eurydice from the shadows into the sunlight of the upper world.

The question is thrust upon us whether the search is even necessary. After all the poems are there for any one to read; they speak directly to our hearts without an intermediary;

every sensitive reader responds to the poetic power of "Melancholy Paths" or the "Sedge Songs" without the critic even dipping his pen in the ink. Perhaps it were better, therefore, that he leave the pen undipped and the paper virgin white. Yet he has a role: the poems spring from a complex of intellectual and emotional factors which, once understood, explains the direction and force of their flow. The critic but hinders the normal process of imaginative assimilation, if he merely piles irrelevant facts, like a barrier reef, between the reader and the poem. His task, if it is to be of any avail, is to discover and reveal the sources from which the poems arose, to trace and define the causes which shaped the total poetic activity, lay bare the values which made the poet live as he lived, write as he wrote. If this vision can be had, and shared, the poems take on a deeper and richer life, even though, as it needs must be, the vision is personal and partial.

All this is difficult enough. But there is another problem. The searcher has the realization thrust upon him that the historical era he has sought and, if fortunate, called again into partial existence as the world of the poet, is completely alien to the age for which he is evoking it. Values and ideals shift; what one age sought, another may spurn. The goals of a poet of one hundred years ago no longer stir the heart today. Of Lenau's age and ours this is unfortunately true. An age which, like ours, measures success in terms of action and acquirement of possessions cannot sympathize with, can, indeed, barely understand, Lenau's belief that success was achieved when a life exclusively devoted to poetry finds fulfillment in the creation of poems and sees in that the full measure of success. Neither goal is in itself unworthy, but they are blind to each other's virtues and have little or no charity for each other's weaknesses.

The problem of understanding Lenau is intensified for us today because the source of his poetry was (to an extent rare even among poets, and the poetic heart is always all from them his creative vitality seemed to draw its strength. His is a poetry of darkness and shadow, a world of melancholy. What is an age like ours to make of such an obsession (the word seems justified) with the threads of suffering which run as strands through the fabric of life but seemed for Lenau to be its total warp and woof? In our youthful buoyancy of spirit (or was that yesterday and not today?), in the joy of action which leaves little time for regrets and sorrows, in a childish fear of accepting the bitterness of life (as if it could all be sweet!), and in the even more childish belief that to deny the existence of life's pain is to destroy it, in our immature faith that we can escape pain and suffering by rushing to the refuge of the psychiatrist's couch when a first hint of their existence appears on the horizon of our spoiled consciousness, we find so melancholy a conception of life not only alien to us but also frightening. So we turn back from Lenau's vision to the blissful world of Pollyanna, neglecting the basic human duty of facing up to life as it is. Even where our present day intellectuals do depict life's pain and suffering, they all too often plunge into an uncreative pessimism so deeply dyed in black as to be as false as its opposite, the shallow optimism of the closed eyes. They lack the buoyancy and courage that were in Lenau's heart, even in the midst of the melancholy that engulfed him. And so they are no closer to understanding him than are the devotees of the Pollyanna cult.

If one is afraid to face the obvious fact that life has, as part of its necessary structure, pain and suffering, sorrow and bitterness, transience and death, and does not realize that without them it cannot go on being a vital process, he needs to come face to face with someone like Lenau. It would be a creative experience, if it were experienced fully, to widen one's field of vision beyond the narrow prospect of the

Hollywood eye view and to learn to face the fact that the Madison-Avenue-created barrier of words, pretty words, cannot halt the storming in of the full and various forces of existence, the bitter as well as the sweet, pain as well as joy, death as well as life. There have been human beings who, touched by some special wizardry of fate, are shut in a narrow range of experience where pain and sadness seem to make up for them, either emotionally or intellectually, the sum total of existence, the Leopardis, the James Thomsons, the Schopenhauers. Narrow as their range is, they explore areas of life that are valid, though not to the exclusion, as they were made to feel, of the other dimensions of existence; and in their exploration they map out areas we must all—no matter how we struggle to travel only the thruways of joy—traverse in our journey from birth to death. It is a part of human dignity not to fear and avoid knowledge of the deserts, the wild mountains, the icy glaciers, the bottomless fens we must cross, but to accept them as part of the creative totality which alone is life. It is thus that our today must read, for its beauty as well as for its insights into melancholy as a valid part of the experience of life, the poetic yesterday (and in a deeper sense the poetic today) of the lyrics of Franz Nikolaus Niembsch Edler von Strehlenau, or rather—a name greater than the full name with its title of nobility included—Nikolaus Lenau, poet.

1.

The story of a life begins not with birth and childhood but with one's national culture, one's ancestors and one's parents. How much Lenau owed to his Hungarian background and his youth in Hungary is impossible to measure exactly; that there is a debt is certain. Even though one may hesitate to ascribe Lenau's temperament to the Hungarian blood in his veins, we know that the world in which one lives as a child leaves lasting impressions which may be overlaid by later influences but are never eradicated. A statement of his friend Anastasius Grün suggests that the influence went deep: in the early days of his insanity Lenau spoke German with a Hungarian accent, "as if he had been transported to the land of his childhood." Grün believes that "the origin and the name of his family point to Slavic ancestry; by birth and upbringing he belongs to the Magyar country . . . ,"and further that "the structure of his cheek bones reveals something of the noble South Slavic type." This is a basic substratum in Lenau's psyche, but it is buried deep under the German element, for, as Grün adds, "by education, way of thinking and the choice of his heart he belongs to the German world." There is little evidence, if any, that there was any conflict between these two disparate influences; Lenau's problem derives from other factors than that he was caught between two national cultures. There is concrete evidence of the Hungarian influence in some of his poems. Indeed, Grün states that Lenau "discovered Hungary for German literature." To a degree this is true, but the dynamic core of Lenau's lyrics is not Hungarian. There are, however, poems dealing with Hungarian subjects: the wild gypsy temperament ("Mischka on the Theiss" and "Mischka on the Marosch"); romantic Hungarian hussars, robbers and peasants; a Danube boatman. The Hungarian steppes are the background for several poems, among others "The Three Gypsies," "The Voice of the Rain," and "Ahasverus, the Wandering Jew." Lenau's Faust compares the wild sea winds to horses galloping across the steppes. In fact, however, it is, if anything, surprising how little Hungarian subject matter Lenau treats rather than how much. The Hungarian element seems to have been minor both in his works and in his life. He was to his Swabian friends the romantic Hungarian nobleman (as, of course, he was) and Lenau may quite understandably have played the role; but he was German-oriented. His restless wanderings never took him east of Vienna. He used whatever subject matter served to give expression to the problems of his tumultuous heart and among the subjects was the Hungarian; it was not, however, primary in his experience or his poetry.

Easier to evaluate is the influence of his parents and his family life as a child. Lenau's mother was a woman of unusually violent emotions, as is revealed in the letters she wrote Lenau's father before their marriage. In them one can see her temperament and her inner tensions in all their violence: her belief that plots were being hatched against her by his family and her threats of suicide. The marriage took place less than a month before the birth of their first daughter, after a stormy period of waiting until Franz von Strehlenau resigned his commission in the army and took a civil service position in order to support his family. Even after the marriage, the emotional tensions did not lessen. Lenau's father, also temperamental, was not only unfaithful to his wife, but also an ardent gambler. One incident is symptomatic: sent one day to a near-by town to bring a doctor to the bedside of his mortally ill daughter, the father, forgetting his mission, got into a gambling session and lost heavily. Instead of the doctor, there came to Lenau's mother at the deathbed of the child the winners bringing the father's IOUs to be co-signed by the despairing mother. Franz von Strehlenau died in his thirtieth year, leaving Lenau's mother a widow whose sole emotional outlet was now her five-year-old son, Nikolaus, a relationship that was not changed but rather probably intensified by her second marriage to the ineffectual Dr. Vogel.

Of his father Lenau has little to say in his letters; nor does one find any suggestion of an emotional attachment in his poems. Where there is mention of a father (one can hardly say his father) as in the "Voice of the Wind," the very indefiniteness of the reference suggests a lack of deep feeling. On the other hand, Lenau's letters to his mother reveal a complete emotional involvement, as do the many poems which center in his love for her, e.g., "Sanctuary" and "The Sick in Heart." As she lay dying, he writes an intimate friend:

> *The sad vision of my mother's fading away will never leave me as long as I live.—I grow more and more frightened, and look around in terror for a heart that will beat for me when this beloved heart is still.—My fate seems to desire to take away from me that which I love, seems to blow out, one after another, the lamps that have till now lighted my dark life, in order that I may be in darkness and go to sleep.*

One of his most violent attacks of depression followed her death. His emotional involvement remained strong even after her death: "I still dream of my mother's deathbed. The memory is carved most deeply into my heart." And again: "I dreamed of my mother today and when I awoke I felt a blissful calm; a kindly star stands above this house; I shall come again soon." Lenau's own relationship to his mother is mirrored in Savonarola's vision after the torture: he meets his mother in heaven, the mother who in the second canto of the poem had worn herself out searching for her lost son, as Lenau's mother had herself done when Nikolaus had once remained out all night with the herdsmen.

Not only the deep emotional involvement with his mother, rooted in her obsessive devotion to him, which at one period made her leave her second husband to be with her son in Vienna, revealed in these and many more instances, is important, but also the fact that, as Eduard Castle points out, she spoiled the boy, who was to her "nature's masterpiece," limitlessly and so developed the boundless vanity which Castle considers one of the basic characteristics of Lenau's personality. As the only son, to whom mother and sisters devoted themselves, eating black bread that he might have cake, he could not but develop an abnormal sense of his own importance. This already emotionally complex relationship was further complicated when Lenau's paternal grandparents insisted on taking the boy into their home and bringing him up. His mother's first reaction was jealous fear that they were plotting to separate her from her idol. When at last she allowed them to have the boy, the strictness of their discipline conflicted violently with his mother's overindulgence and led to further emotional problems. These tangled emotional tensions worked together in the heart of the extremely impressionable boy to form the indelible pattern of the tumultuous heart, of the temperament which was to be the source of Lenau's melancholy and of his lyrical genius.

When Lenau reached the age when he had to make his own decisions as to his future and undertake his university studies, a trait that was to mark his whole life appeared: his inability to attach himself to a place or a profession. He might have said with his "Wandering Jew" (he wrote two poems on this theme): "Only I of all mortals can in my unhappiness find no rest." The story of Lenau's life is in large part the story of restless wandering. The tendency first revealed itself as symptomatic of a deep psychological trend when he began his university studies and changed from university to university and from one field of study to another: philosophy in Vienna, Hungarian law in Pressburg and the same autumn a change to Ungarisch Altenberg to study agricultural economics; the next spring he took up the study of German law in Vienna and soon after began the study of medicine at the same university. This course of study he followed from 1826 to 1830, until, upon his grandmother's death in 1830, he no longer needed to carry on studies that satisfied her who held the purse strings and could, with the money he inherited from her, lead a life without any professional activity. He now began the truly nomadic existence which was to continue until his final illness. In 1831 he journeyed to Stuttgart, in part to advance his literary career by contacting the Swabian group of poets (Justinus Kerner, Gustav Schwab, the Hartmanns and the Reinbecks) and to find a publisher for his poems, which he could not publish under the Austrian censorship, and in part to finish his medical studies at Heidelberg. In Swabia he found congenial friends and a second home, to which he returned over and over again, continually traveling for the rest of his life between Stuttgart and Vienna, since, for various reasons, he found it impossible to settle in either place permanently. He found a publisher in the famous firm of Cotta and warm understanding and flattering admiration from the Swabian poets. His study of medicine in Heidelberg was, however, desultory and fruitless.

In 1832 Lenau undertook his most adventurous journey, his trip to and in the United States, an experience which seems to have been surprisingly unproductive and unhappy, possibly because of ill health, possibly because of disillusionment with the world of reality which did not correspond to the exaggeratedly ideal picture he had conjured up in his mind (he even thought he should find monkeys in the American forests). During the American journey Lenau was, indeed, not well (possibly to the extent of a neurasthenic breakdown, as Vincenzo Errante believes). He seems also to have undertaken the trip in a wildly romantic spirit; as one biographer puts it: "a twelve-year-old schoolboy whose imagination had been fired to the boiling point by garishly colored Indian stories could not have acted more romantically, more fantastically and irrationally than did the usually sharp-sighted poet." The motives that led him to undertake the journey were varied: his discontent with political conditions in Europe, especially in Austria, and his admiration for American political freedom; a desire to increase his income by investing in land; the unhappiness caused by his renunciation of Lotte Gmelin; and, above all, his desire to enrich his poetic development by new experiences. None of these purposes was achieved. He was soon completely disillusioned, as his letters home reveal, disillusioned with American democracy (which he considered selfishness in action, a mere form of property insurance); with the dollar-minded, bustling Americans and especially with American women who, he felt, lacked soul (*Gemüt*); with the climate and the scenery. The fact that America had no nightingales seemed to him a symbol of all the shortcomings he observed. One is tempted to say, with the necessary changes, what Heine said of London: "For Heaven's sake, send a philosopher, but not a lyric poet to London!" One is also inclined to feel that Lenau's view was completely jaundiced, until one remembers Dicken's portrayal of the United States in *Martin Chuzzlewit,* and begins to wonder whether Lenau did not see more clearly than one had at first thought. Financially Lenau had difficulties; before the Rhine steamer had reached Holland, he and his fellow passengers had discovered the fraudulent nature of the German Emigration Society in which they had invested their capital. In this respect, his American journey was a disappointment.

His desire to enrich his poetic development was in some measure achieved, though not, as he had expected, through romantic experiences in an exotic world, but rather—and this is typical of Lenau—through an intensification of his melancholy. He had expected to find a "tremendous wealth of the most glorious scenes" which, as yet as virgin and unexploited as the primeval forests, would, he felt, bring him poetic inspiration. "I promise my self marvelous effects from these things on my soul (*Gemüt*)." Even here he was disappointed; only three things impressed him deeply: Niagara Falls, the scenery along the Hudson River and the primeval forest. In general, he writes, "nature here has no soul and no phantasy and can therefore give neither of these things to its creatures." "Nature here is frighteningly dull." In his disillusionment, he asks himself why he ever came. "And yet," he writes,

"I do know why. John baptized in the wilderness. I too was drawn into the wilderness and here in my inmost being something like baptism has really taken place." In his loneliness, without friends, in the midst of a "soulless" nature, he has, he claims, been brought to a better understanding of himself and to the attainment of decisions which will be important for his future life. That any real change and development took place is highly doubtful; the American journey did not change the melancholy orientation which was the core of his existence.

The American journey, the extreme case of Lenau's tendency to the nomadic life, was an unsuccessful experiment which, although he considered and talked of a second trip, he never repeated. Escape into a new and different world did not solve the problems of his tumultuous heart. Lenau was to remain throughout his life a wanderer, but his wanderings were henceforward limited to the journey between Stuttgart and Vienna.

The poetic harvest of the American journey is not a rich one. There are poems depicting the tragedy of the Indians driven from their homes by the white men, a theme that was neither new nor given by Lenau a treatment worthy of his lyric genius, and a poem or two on Niagara. In only two poems does he give full expression to his emotional inner life and achieve a level of poetic power typical of his genius but still not in his highest range. The nature setting in both "The Block House" and "The Primeval Forest" is fused with a typical melancholy to reveal his inner being. The source of his best American poems, the poetically most creative experience of the whole journey, was his discovery of the ocean. "The ocean has taken possession of my heart," he writes. "The two chief factors in nature that have shaped my being are the Atlantic Ocean and the Austrian Alps." There are five of these poems in the section of his collected works called "Atlantica" and a few later sea poems like

"Ocean's Silence." One does not feel in any of them, however, the radiance of his full genius. After all, he concluded the above statement by admitting: "I should call myself, however, pre-eminently the pupil of the latter."

For Nikolaus Lenau the verb *to live* was, one might well say, spelled with an *o* and not an *i*. Throughout his life, love was a central experience, the source from which most of his poetry flowed, fusing with his intimate relationship to the world of nature to give life to his loveliest lyrics. His restless wandering was closely connected with his love affairs. Women, indeed, played a major role in his life, from his early devotion to his mother to his attempt to find happiness with Marie Behrends just before his final breakdown. He was extremely dependent emotionally on his sister Therese, as his letters reveal; he found in Emilie Reinbeck, one of his Swabian friends, a continual source of consolation, strength and inspiration. It was she who helped him combat his periods of depression and nursed him in the first stages of his breakdown. To her he wrote some of his most revealing letters and first sent many of his poems.

Lenau's earliest love affair, that with Bertha Hauer, who is probably best described by the Viennese phrase "ein süsses Mädel," (one whose heart overrules her head), when he was a student in Vienna, did not, like his later affairs, confront him with the problem of remaining free from the bonds of middle-class domesticity for the sake of his poetic career. It was his closest approach to *la vie de Bohème*. It does reveal his tendency, from which derived much of his melancholy, to idealize reality and then wake up to the true facts with shattering disillusionment. He created a falsely romanticized image of Bertha, a very ordinary example of her class, and then, when he discovered her true character, suffered more deeply than the situation warranted. At first he was ecstatically happy in having found and won what he thought was innocent loveliness; then suddenly he learned that she was a creature of very common clay. On a sensitive and imaginative nature like Lenau's such an experience has a traumatic effect. His poetry takes on greater intensity and depth of feeling. In a sense, he exploited his experience for his poetic purposes, i.e., he drew from it the last drop of sweetness and pain and for this reason kept it alive long after the non-poet would have forgotten it.

The next two love affairs show Lenau trying unsuccessfully to reconcile his love with his need for freedom to follow his poetic career. In the first case, that of Nanette Wolf, there was little or no struggle; it created a poem or two and was soon over. His love for Lotte Gmelin and his renunciation of her affected him deeply and was the source of some of his loveliest lyrics, the "Sedge Songs." Lenau felt instinctively that he could not settle down in a middle-class existence, take up a profession and no longer be able to devote himself exclusively to his poetry. The renunciation created far-reaching tensions; he loved her and suffered deeply, but he could not betray his lyric muse. This is clearly revealed in his anger at the pressure brought to bear by her cousins, the Schwabs, to make him declare his intention of marrying her. It is clear also in his worry about his financial position; to marry Lotte he would have had to have a secure income and tie himself down to a definite profession; this he could not bring himself to do. At times he wavered; his American journey was planned in part to bring him financial gain and make the marriage with her possible. The emotional conflict led to one of his periods of deepest melancholy, the worst since the death of his mother and the ending of the affair with Bertha. To this melancholy he ascribes his inability to marry Lotte: "I shall renounce this girl, for I feel so little happiness within me that I can give none to others." Because of his melancholy, he fears "to fasten this heavenly rose (Lotte) to my night-dark heart." He writes: "I love the girl endlessly. But my inner being is sadness and my love painful renunciation." Lenau saw clearly that his poetic temperament made it impossible for him to marry a simple and unsophisticated girl like Lotte; his melancholy and his tendency to exploit everything for his poetic purposes would only make her unhappy.

His love for Sophie von Löwenthal, which he calls one of the four major influences on his poetic development (the others are the ocean, the Alps, and Beethoven) dominated his life from the end of 1833 to his collapse in 1844. The problem in this case was not that of safeguarding his freedom as poet, but the frustration of unfulfilled desires. Sophie von Löwenthal was married and had children; her husband was Lenau's friend. Evidently a woman of great charm, known in her circle as "the irresistible one," probably not emotionally satisfied in her marriage, used to being courted and adored, she found Lenau's love a source of satisfaction otherwise unattainable and gloried in being loved by the famous and popular poet. On the other hand, she never gave up her family and her social position for Lenau and was careful not to compromise herself in her relations with him. Lenau critics differ widely in their judgments of her character and motives; some hold that she was a coquette who, not caring for Lenau's sufferings, manipulated and exploited him for her own purposes and destroyed him in the process; others believe that she, like Lenau, was one of "love's martyrs" who could not live without him any more than he could without her. That she caused him to suffer in spite of the happiness she gave him is beyond question. She awoke his passions and yet frustrated them by denying them full satisfaction; she fascinated him and then again drove him to try to escape from an unbearable situation. The whole story is best told in the letters Lenau wrote her, of which he himself says: "These notes are to me the most precious things I have written. Any one who wants to know me must read them." In them one can clearly see Lenau's passion and unhappiness. "You have become so completely the extreme goal of my wishes and emotions that my yearning can turn from you only to death." "Passions have eaten away at my life, my last passion most of all." "I shall love you eternally, but I shall lock my emotions within my autumnal loneliness." "I should die, that is certain, (if I lost you). If God takes you from me, He takes away the very basis of my existence; He takes away food and drink from my heart; He takes away the air which I breathe; He does not want me to go on living." "I am truly sick—I think continually of you and death." "Love is the strongest power in heaven and on earth; it created the world and preserves it and causes it to move eternally; it has taken possesion of our hearts and all that is contrary to love must burn up and be annihilated, like a straw cast into a burning volcano."

The intensity of his passion and the continual frustration that short-circuited the current were an unbearable strain on Lenau. "You are terribly wrong if you think there are moments when I love you less. I love you always. But there is a darkening, a fading of my spiritual (*geistigen*) powers which I cannot describe." "I could weep when I think how my powers are declining without our ever being able to hold each other fully in a close embrace." The depression deepens and the physical symptoms intensify: "I am in the most wretched mood: that irritable disgust, that giving up of all hope for, and joy in, the future." "An abominable depression has been hounding me for days." "A severe languor, depression and irritability which verges at times on the violent, these are my major attributes at the moment." "Like a November day on the Hungarian steppes is the mood that lies on my heart. Everything I undertake and do is inexpressibly desert and empty and stale. My earthly life has a hole in it through which the best part falls. I lack you. . . ." The tension becomes unbearable; his situation resembles "the tortures of hell," but the tortures are more sophisticated than any hell can inflict. He wavers, he writes, between depression and overstimulated gaiety. "We gamble with the world, we cheat it, and it will nail our hands to the table. I should gladly die right now. I feel strongly that I am ripe for death. There is a tumult in me. My life seems extremely suspect to me. It is roasting me at a slow fire. My life is tricky, it is a traitor." And yet he cannot renounce his love: "I have never dreamed of a joy for which I would exchange this unhappiness. A glimpse into your soul is not too dearly bought with the most painful renunciation, even though it means a struggle to the day of my death." "(Your love) binds me to the world and to myself; without it all would break apart." "It is no empty flattery when I tell you that I cannot live without you. I say it in deadly earnest," he writes when he hears that she has been ill. "Our love has been my saving, my salvation, but now it stands face to face with me so powerfully that I am frightened." He will not let even his poetry bring him relief: "I would gladly trample my works underfoot, if they ever imagined that they were comforting me for your not being mine." There come moments, however, as in 1838, when he let the correspondence with her lapse for a month, when he seems, in self-defense, to desire "not to evoke a painful depression which might well carry me too far. I probably should, for our love's sake, spare my heart and with it my life." And yet he cannot give her up: "If I were to lose you, I see myself wandering astray in the future, a man lost beyond rescue and breaking down completely." "It is the nature of love," he writes, "that it not only fills the lover's breast but also the whole world, like the air one breathes." It is the source from which his lyrics flow; when separated from her, he writes, "I work with only half my soul." It has become his whole existence: "This love—is no longer in me; I am in it. It is my god." His inescapable doom intensifies his nervous condition: "The devil take my nerves. Or rather he has taken them already and sometimes he strings them on his violin and plays me ghastly melodies on them."

Twice he attempted to escape from the painful bliss or the blissful pain of his love. In 1839 he became engaged to the well-known actress and singer Karoline Unger; in 1844, to a young girl of simple middle-class background, Marie Behrends. His letters to Sophie von Löwenthal show all too plainly that neither attempt could possibly have succeeded. Thus, the note in which he tells her of his engagement to Karoline Unger ends: "If you withdraw your love from me, you give me my death blow; if you are unhappy, I will die. The knot is drawn tight. I would I were already dead." "I have been really sick these last few days. I must find some solution. Do not abandon me now." And again: "I will accept the law of my life and my whole fate from your heart which has never seemed greater and more holy than it does in your last letter; a mountain of woe lies on my breast. The way of escape you suggest leads through the gateway of my death." It is small wonder that the affair with Karoline Unger was soon broken off. The second attempt follows a similar course. He writes to Marie Behrends after their meeting in Baden-Baden and his offer of marriage that she has performed a miracle by bringing him a feeling of peace and joy in life and has re-awakened his courage, that their meeting has given him a final chance to achieve a reconciliation with life and find salvation. A few weeks later, however, he is assuring Sophie von Löwenthal that she is, and shall remain, his muse and that it is unthinkable that an intimate connection with her could ever cease, that she is indispensable to his mind and heart. He will, he writes, "stick loyally and firmly to the text of your golden letter which shall be a law to me." "My attitude toward you, dear Sophie," he adds, "is unchangeable, ensured and dedicated by deepest suffering." In his next letter, he writes: "You shall lose nothing, even if my marriage does take place."

The letters reveal the insoluble dilemma which Lenau

faced, and show that the attempts to free himself only intensified the emotional turmoil. While the affair with Sophie von Löwenthal bore rich fruit in his lyrics, it proved too violent, too frustrating, too hopeless, and tore to pieces the poet who lived in its cyclonic tumult. The lively poetic activity of these years must have served as a partial release from the tensions, for he was able to bear the situation for ten years; and yet the poems could not completely save him. His unhappy love for Sophie von Löwenthal was not the sole cause, but certainly a contributory cause of his complete breakdown in 1844, when insanity brought a tragic ending to Lenau's poetic career. He died in 1850.

2.

As a man and as a poet, Lenau reveals a paradoxical combination of strength of character and romantic turbulence of emotion. Lenau was a man of strong principles and complete integrity of character; this is one side of his nature. He defines the other when he writes of a contemporary poet, Georg Herwegh: "He . . . has talent, but no chaos. There is (in him) no primeval world which struggles toward form." Lenau had both integrity, principles, and strength of character on the one hand and also, on the other, the creative "chaos," "the primeval world," of the tumultuous heart. He was a man of tremendous overpowering temperament, with emotions so turbulent that they continuously shook his world to its foundations, and, at the same time, a man who, underneath the chaotic surface, was no moral weakling, no mere victim of life, but its master, devoting himself to the fulfillment of his life's purpose, his vocation as poet. "I am hard and proud enough to despise misfortune," he writes. "I have once and for all taken my stand vis-à-vis life; it shall not get me down. That my resistance is not that of the calm philosopher but has much stubborn defiance in it is due to my temperament. I shall be able to master it (my life)." At first glance, Lenau's romantic turbulence and his suggestibility and sensitivity seem to outweigh the stronger side of his nature. But there is an inner consistency and integrity in his life and works which justify Max von Löwenthal's statement that "he stands unique among our poets in the nobility of his soul, in his unbending independence of spirit. . . ." There was, indeed, in Lenau a sense of direction, a courage, an integrity which lay like rocks in the midst of the swirling, storm-driven breakers. Lenau's poetry rests on a sure foundation of purposeful integrity; those who were closest to him knew he was not the victim of a directionless confusion.

And yet Lenau is the temperamental poet, indeed almost the archetype of the temperamental poet. "A temperament like mine," he writes, "brings with it a retinue of sufferings but also of joys of which the comfortable, pedantic plodders have no conception." Emilie Reinbeck writes that his constitution was delicate and extremely sensitive (*reizbar*); that he tended to melancholy which, she believes, must have objective causes in a man of his basically firm character; that he lacked control over impressions and moods; that he was full of contradictions. Other friends also noted his extreme suggestibility and sensitivity: "I know of no one whose facial expression, skin color and bearing change so much with mood as do Lenau's; a slight illness, especially bodily pain (a headache, a toothache), a sleepless night or an upsetting letter made him look yellow and withered, brought out deep wrinkles, bowed him down." Another writes: "I have never seen any one in whom impressions go so deep; when something moved him deeply, often just listening to lovely music, he could not eat a bite." His reactions were not only sensitive and violent; they also changed rapidly: he "could let himself go gaily and laugh heartily; the next minute his face would be transformed and become rigid and deeply melancholy." Joined to his sensitivity and suggestibility in an inextricable tangle is an unusually keen poetic imagination, a tendency to enlarge, to dramatize, to intensify, to "exploit" his experiences. He describes the process in a letter to Sophie von Löwenthal:

> *The violence of my passion seems to have an uncanny quality in my own eyes. My mistake is that I do not keep the sphere of poetry and the sphere of real life apart but let the two become entangled. Accustomed to surrender myself to the drive of my imagination in my poetry, I do the same thing in life, and so it comes about that in moments of self-forgetfulness this power, probably too well exercised, builds itself up and tramples destructively on its own fairest creations.*

"I am in general a poor manager and in the economy of my psychological powers I keep too lax an accounting, too little balance and order." "The sudden shift of my moods from highest bliss to deepest melancholy reveals to me the pathological tension of my soul." To live thus is to live dangerously; and Lenau lived thus. Only the strong character that lay beneath the surface kept him from disaster.

The basic mood of Lenau's life and poetry is melancholy. "I am a melancholist. The compass needle of my soul ever vibrates back to the pain of life." "The divine in life has never appeared to me without the accompaniment of sadness." "Melancholy was united in him with the will to pain. The latter is the driving force in his life and poetry; certainly not as a conscious intention but as an unconscious (*dunkler*) urge which told him that he needed pain as the source of his dark poetry," writes Heinrich Bischoff, one of the most careful students of his life and works. As another critic writes: "He recognizes that he possesses the talent for pain which, as Ibsen says, a poet must possess." Pain and melancholy were for him, indeed, the primary stimuli to poetic creation; the flower of his lyrics grew from their dark soil in rich profusion. His poetry is intimately linked with the frequent attacks of depression that at times went to the point of "temporary madness" and led to thoughts of suicide, e.g., after his mother's death, after his disillusionment with Bertha, and repeatedly during the affair with Sophie von Löwenthal. Bischoff sums the situation up: "Pain was his heritage; his life experience, his life's element; it became the purpose of his life. He made it his profession and developed an incomparable skill in cherishing it; he reveled in it to the point of ecstacy." Melancholy designed, indeed, the basic pattern in the tapestry of his life; *Weltschmerz,* an all too keen awareness of the pain in individual and universal life, dominated his existence.

The causes of this unique quality of Lenau's poetic genius lie deeply buried in his psychological heritage and in the emotional turbulence of his childhood experiences, and defy facile interpretation. He himself explained his melancholy as the result of a "break" or "tear" in his psyche, some traumatic experience that left an ineradicable mark on his personality; but his statements are so cryptic and ambiguous as to be of little help in explaining the phenomenon. It was, in any case, intensified by his hypersensitive and suggestible nature and the all too vivid poetic imagination that exaggerated and dramatized every experience he underwent, turning every pain into an agony, every sorrow into a paroxysm of woe, every transient hurt into a lasting wound. And finally, it derived in large measure from his dedication to his poetic calling, a dedication which demanded the exploitation of every experience for the purposes of his lyric mission.

Among the major forces, indeed, which shaped Lenau's life, giving it definition and content, was his conception of himself as a poet (we all live the life of the person we conceive ourselves to be). His self-dedication to the role of lyric singer of his experiences made any other activity, profession or a settled Philistine life impossible for him. He was fortunate that his financial independence, after he received his grandmother's inheritance, freed him from any such need. From that time on, he allowed nothing to interfere with the overpowering urge to follow his poetic career. "Is lyric poetry," he writes, "not your dearest love, you perhaps ask. No, I cannot call it a love; I think poetry is I myself; my self-most self is poetry." "To cherish my artistic development is the highest goal in life; I look upon all the powers of my mind, the happiness of my soul (*Gemüt*), as means to this end." To illustrate his meaning, he cites a poem by Adalbert von Chamisso in which a painter nails a youth to the cross in order to study pain for his artistic purposes; and continues: "I will nail myself to the cross, if that will produce a good poem. He who does not risk everything for the sake of his art is not honest with his art. Art is care and a great deal of work. Schiller is wrong when he says that 'life is serious; art is gay.' I see more seriousness in art than in life, where all is transitory, joy and pain, whereas in art all is enduring and eternal." "I should not be worthy of the slightest favor from the immortal muse, if I were not able to sacrifice everything gladly to her service, all my happiness and all my joys." Even as a young man he was convinced that "all the pleasures which money, office, etc., can give" are of little worth compared to "the bliss one feels when one carries his own world within himself."

It is this high conception of his poetic calling that gives form and direction to Lenau's whole life. He believed that total dedication was demanded of the human being chosen to serve the muse of poetry; there can be no question of part-time and leisure-time service; poetry must be the central and not the peripheral activity. One cannot serve both Erato and Mercury. It was his high conception of his poetic calling which made it impossible for him to settle into a normal, middle-class existence, to marry either Nanette Wolf or

Lotte Gmelin, to become a professor of aesthetics, as he at one time thought of doing, or a doctor. It was because of this that he cherished and exploited his own emotions, especially his own unhappiness, as a source of poetic inspiration. This conception of his poetic purpose spread like an indelible stain from the center of his being and colored everything to the very edges of his existence.

For an observer to whom poetry is not a matter of such high seriousness, a question of life and death, an all-encompassing self-dedication, it is easy to look upon Lenau's actions and reactions in a very different light, to see them as weak self-pity, as a pose, as an expression of vanity striving to impress those around him. Thus, even Eduard Castle, greatest of the Lenau scholars, feels that Lenau "could have gotten over" the unhappiness of the affair with Bertha Hauer, if his vanity had not made him continually tear the wound open in order to make himself an interesting figure in the eyes of his friends. He held so firmly to the pose, says Castle, that it finally became a matter of deadly earnest. It is true that Lenau "exploited" this experience, as he did every experience, but he did not do so to make himself an interesting and romantic figure in the eyes of his Swabian friends. On the contrary, he was "nailing himself to the cross" because, only by so exploiting his experience, could he create as a poet and so fulfill what was to him the central purpose of his life. Hermann Engelhard in his recent edition of Lenau's works and letters comes much closer to a correct evaluation of Lenau's motives: "That poetry is self-sacrifice he (Lenau) considers its best attribute and he has indeed the right to assert of himself: 'My complete works are my complete life.' " The development of his poetic purpose and the course of his life are completely intertwined. "With unequalled lack of restraint Lenau pays his vows to his poetic way of life." An illustration of his exploiting experience for the sake of his poetry is to be found in his explanation of the purpose of the American journey: "I need America for my cultural development. There I shall send my imagination to school, to the school of the primeval forests. But I shall also torture my heart in my yearning for my beloved (Lotte Gmelin)." What at first glance seems a pose, the playing of a romantic role, a strutting vanity or even an indulging himself in self-pity, flowed in reality from his conception of his poetic purpose and his willingness, or rather his urgent need, to feed his poetry with his own life blood. He was a dedicated man who, because he was a poet, had no choice but to exploit his experiences as the source of his lyrics.

This conception of his poetic calling involved Lenau in a very modern dilemma: the problematic relationship between the poet and the Philistine life around him. In Lenau's day the problem had not yet been fully defined nor become as acute as it was to become in the last decades of the nineteenth century. Lenau himself was not fully conscious of the problem and could not define it in modern terms, but it was none the less one of his problems. The gap between poet and life as it is lived by the normal, non-poetic individual had not as yet become in Germany an impassable gulf; it was still the world of Theodor Storm and not that of Thomas Mann. The solution of the problem by escape into *la vie de Bohème* had not yet become the accepted goal; there was as yet no conscious flight to a poetic *rive gauche* from everyday bourgeois existence. And yet the story of Lenau's life suggests that he was caught between his life as a dedicated poet and the middle-class existence of which he was a part. In a real sense he needed a world where poetry was the *sine qua non* of existence and he instinctively sought it; here may well lie a partial explanation of his wandering life. On the other hand, he accepted the middle-class world as he found it in Stuttgart and Vienna and did not really try to find any other type of existence. His Swabian friends led stable middle-class lives; their poetry was superimposed on their normal life. And in Vienna, Sophie von Löwenthal and her civil-servant husband led a strictly middle-class existence, as is revealed in her skillful manipulation of her relations with Lenau to achieve the adoration she wanted from him and the glory it brought her to be adored by the famous poet and yet never compromise herself in the eyes of "the world." As a career poet, Lenau himself could not fully accept such a settled Philistine life; he needed to have freedom and always preserved his freedom, never tying himself down with wife, family and a profession. Yet he was too much part of it, shared too much its values, to challenge the middle-class world and its goals; but he was still always instinctively on guard against being swallowed up into it.

The period of his life which comes closest to *la vie de Bohème* is that of his student days in Vienna and his affair with Bertha Hauer; but the freedom of student days does not last forever. He avoided marriage with Lotte Gmelin because he knew it meant the acceptance of a middle-class way of life and hence a danger to his poetic career. On the other hand, it is evident in his affair with the singer Karoline Unger, if Max von Löwenthal's account is to be trusted, that Lenau was not at home in the world of the professional artist. He was upset by her temperamental demands that he, on whom up till now women had always waited hand and foot, should play the role of servitor. He was distressed when she, a woman of violent and theatrical emotions, with a "past," flaunted her affair with him in the public eye with complete disregard for "what the world thought." He even feared that her love for him might not be genuine but merely theatrical, and was easily susceptible, therefore, to the hints dropped by Sophie von Löwenthal concerning her rival which combined with his own reactions to the ways of a professional and temperamental artist to bring a speedy ending to the affair.

Lenau was more at home in the middle-class world than he was in the world of the theater and the prima donna.

The affair with Karoline Unger reveals Lenau caught between the Philistine world in which he lived and to which, indeed, he felt akin, though he could not accept it fully, and the world of the professional artist where he was not at home. His attitude is ambivalent; in letter after letter he praises middle-class life and admits his need for it and then again instinctively struggles against its demands and criticizes it. "Philistinism," he writes, "is more destructive to the poet than despotism. The latter stimulates him; the former wears him down." "It is Philistinism and its pedantry which keeps poetry from growing freely." This ambivalence is to be found throughout his life. There was no German Paris to which he could flee, even if he had wanted to; the café life of Vienna was no escape from middle-class life but a mere phase of it. The world of the aristocracy offered him no avenue of escape, for, according to a friend, he "kept himself remote from the life of courts and the higher social circles as a matter of principle." He told his friend most revealingly: "I do not want to be exceptional, I do not want to have these foolish poetic freedoms."

For a man and a poet of strong character such as Lenau, whose dynamic center is within himself, the philosophical and literary influences which impinge upon him are at once transformed—or cast aside; they are not without influence but the influence is of brief duration and the transformation rapid and complete. Neither the trend of his thought nor the subject matter and form of his lyrics can be explained, therefore, by citing philosophers studied or lyric forerunners read. Lenau studied Spinoza in Heidelberg; he fell under the spell of the Danish theologian H. L. Martensen, during the writing of *Savonarola,* and under that of Hegel while creating *Die Albigenser;* he responded now and again to other philosophical influences. Yet these do not form the molten core of his lyric creativity. A poet of Lenau's type takes from philosophers only what is needed and can be made use of by the inner self, detached ideas related to his personal experience rather than the total philosophical system; what he does take is then largely thrown off by the centrifugal force generated by the poetic powers at work within him. A clue to passing phases in his development may lie here, therefore, not the clue to the lasting and formative core of his existence. This is true also of literary influences. Lenau's earliest poems show the influence of the eighteenth century German poets Hölty and Klopstock, but their influence was temporary as he created the personal lyric form he needed. They touched the circle of his poetic life; they did not intersect it. The influence of the romantic school, to which he is closely akin and certainly owes much, at most helps explain trends in his poetry; it too was absorbed into his personal mode of being, into the central dynamic of his personality; he has much that is romantic in him but even more that is Lenau. This interpretation is borne out by the fact that the question of such influences tends to arise largely in connection with his longer, less successful and often atypical epic or dramatic works which, as one of his latest biographers, Vincenzo Errante, points out, represent a wandering into a cul de sac from which Lenau fortunately returned to his true metier, the creation of such lyrics as the "Forest Songs."

Lenau's relationship to the social and political problems of his age reveals him as independent and courageous but tells little about the basic trend of his poetry. He wrote poems glorifying the Polish exiles and their heroic revolution; he inveighed bitterly against the Metternich regime ("At the Grave of a Minister"); he detested the censorship in Austria (after all, Lenau is a pen name designed to hide his identity from the censors). His discontent with political conditions made him think of emigrating to the United States as early as 1830 and probably played a part in his final decision to undertake the journey. The reactionary age in which he lived awoke his independent spirit to rebellion, but it could not change the lyric poet Lenau into a party-line propagandist. In *Die Albigenser* freedom of thought and spirit is praised and the struggle of the heretics depicted as a stage in Europe's development toward political freedom which is not yet ended. Even in *Savonarola,* the epic poem in which Lenau attacks the Renaissance glorification of the heathen classics and of the senses and also the contemporary Young German cult of the "rehabilitation of the flesh," Savonarola eloquently pleads with the dying Lorenzo to grant political freedom to his subjects. Lenau's personal experience of American democracy at work repelled him and "cured" him of many of his idealistic youthful beliefs. He is, he says in "Protest," a monarchist, although he has no love for "what we possess at the moment in the way of kings" and can still burn with indignation where he sees a prince in his arrogance trample on a people's rights. In this he resembles Heinrich Heine (whom he admired as a poet) who also called himself a monarchist and refused to follow the party line of contemporary German liberalism. Of the politically minded Young Germans he had little good to say. In the last analysis, Lenau's political attitude has its roots not in ideas but in the admirably independent and honest character of the man himself. His conception of himself as a lyric poet kept him from ever subordinating poetry to politics; he had to be free (and this for him was the ultimate freedom) to formulate in his lyrics his experience of life as his genius demanded. Poetry says, in "Poetry and Her Disturbers," to those who would have her serve political or social ends, that such activity is to her suspect; she must have freedom to follow her native bent; only by so doing can she serve the cause of true freedom which the rustling of the leaves in the forest proclaims more clearly "than the leaves of your journals and all your soulless cackle of words."

The problem of being a poet in this sense in an age that was almost completely politically oriented strikes Lenau forcibly. "Our age is not an age for poetry," he writes, "only politics counts. What am I? I am like a stone lying on a desert steppe." "Today the poet cannot be happy," since the age wants not words but political action. "It has pronounced a harsh sentence of banishment on the poet . . ." At other moments he sees a creative element in the confusion of the age and is confident that it is the prelude to a better era. "Our age suffers from a certain degree of impotence as far as matters of the ideal are concerned—perhaps world history desires to lay first a sound industrial-material basis on which some day it can work out its great idealistic conflicts." Looking thus at the world around him, he explains "its dark melancholy," "its anger, its haste and the extreme confusion (*Zerrissenheit*) of the contemporary soul" as due to the fact that those who suffer in the present turmoil and work for a better world cannot experience the achievement of the goal they seek but die "in the dawn" without seeing "the full golden rays of freedom shine." Lenau needed and wanted a climate of political freedom; he was, however, so swept along by the central urge of his being, the need to experience all the varied aspects of life and recreate the experience in poetry, that the political sphere, though it touched the periphery, could never become the central area of his life's activity.

3

Lenau's poetry is, then, the unique expression of a man whose tumultuous heart and extremely vivid imagination swept him through a life marked by the violence of his reactions to the world around him, to his own emotions, to his loves. His poetic activity was, moreover, consciously and unconsciously, the purpose of his existence, a whirlpool into which every phase of his life was drawn. The subject matter of the poems in which these dynamic forces find expression is on the one hand the inner world of the self and on the other the world of nature. The fusion of the two is Lenau's personal and unique achievement. "Observation of human life in its manifold phenomena is in my eyes the greatest stimulus which nature has for me. The latter remains my dearest love, and anyway human life is only an image of nature as the latter is reflected in the tumultuous waves of our impulses."

Lenau's poetic purpose was not to seek out and "enumerate" picturesque details of nature or draw didactic parallels between nature and man's life in a rationalistic fashion; such aims he considered unpoetic. He sought to unite his emotional inner world and the world of external nature so completely that they are brought "into a collision (*Konflikt*) from which then the poet can create a third organically alive sphere." "In the last analysis, only nature and genuinely human emotions are the subjects of true poetry. And yet the wretched contemporary critics cannot despise enough this so-called subjective poetry." Neither the critics nor his own involvement with ideas in such works as *Die Albigenser* and *Savonarola* could keep Lenau from finding the poetic field to which his innate genius was best adapted. In the "Sedge Songs" and the "Forest Songs," Lenau gave an illustration of his theory and purpose that silences all criticism as only true genius can silence it.

Lenau did not discover nature as a poetic subject; nor was he the first poet to link the human heart and the world of nature. Gray and Thomson and their German imitators had already made nature the subject of poetic treatment, though they tended to "enumerate" and, in accord with the rationalism of their age, to draw moralistic parallels between man and nature. Storm and Stress in the eighteenth century and romanticism in the nineteenth went further than this and opened up wider and wilder aspects of nature to the poet and linked him and it in an emotional communion; often, however, they fell into what Ruskin calls the "pathetic fallacy," transferring human emotions to the non-human. Lenau could, and did, draw on a rich heritage of nature poetry, often, as he himself realized, sinning against his own theories, as, for example, in "Heaven's Mourning" where his melancholy is transferred to heaven itself which

. . . by its bitter sorrow stricken
Lets weary fall the sun from out its hand.

When he achieves his purpose, as he does in the "Sedge Songs," however, he does not transfer his emotions into nature but fuses man's emotion and nature in symbols. He uses, as in "Autumn Mood," a human image to describe the autumnal aspect of nature: the beech wood is like "someone sick and on the verge of dying" past whose sickroom the brooklet runs silently, "the final dream of life not now disturbing." The poet himself, however, is not the sick man. Because he is separate from, yet parallel to, autumnal nature, he can realize the similarity of nature's case with his own and yet remain enough apart to see nature as something outside himself with which he can share his mood:

From nature too the last joys now have vanished;
With her into the realm of sadness banished,
He finds that he is part of all her sadness.

In the "Sedge Songs" there is transference of human emotion into nature: the willows are sad, the sedges quake in the wind, the winds lament that the stars are no longer reflected in the storm-tossed lake, "twilight shrouds the trees in sadness," and the whispers in the reeds are sad; but these moods are presented as inherent in nature and independent of the poet; because of this, they can affect him

Till my own tears rise and flow.

This can happen only because he himself is separate from them. His sadness, his sense of the presence of his beloved in the shining of "the lovely evening star" parallels the loveliness of the natural scene; his awareness of his loss of her as he looks on the stormy lake in which the winds seek vainly the reflection of the stars runs parallel to what is happening in nature:

Your love shines upon me never,
Never lights my bitter woe.

The melancholy sighs of the breeze which he hears by the "sedge-lined bayside" as they die into silence against the background of the wide water, exist in their own right and are not her voice; but so similar are they that he now feels that he hears her loved voice dying away "lost in the dark waters' flow." The storm rages and the lightnings are suddenly reflected in the black water; just so, in the dark of his sorrow, her image flashes clearly before him with her hair blowing in the wild winds. The utter calm of the moonlit night lies before him and suddenly thoughts of her fill his being

Like a prayer at eventide.

"Delusion" illustrates the point clearly: the call of the owl, the lightning, the raindrops, the loud winds trapped in the rocky gorge, as they fuse together in a "mighty chorus," all have an objective existence apart from the poet's emotions; he realizes, as an objective fact of nature, that they merely happen at the same time and do not represent a communication of emotion to each other, that "all, all are lonely voices." Exactly so in the human case, "our laments are monologues." The natural and the human move on parallel courses; the natural can, therefore, become the symbol of the human. The natural and the human, just because they are separate yet kindred entities, can enter into a complete fusion in a poetic image. In his finest poems nature is not treated allegorically (as he himself occasionally treats it); it is not in this sense parallel to the human but in the sense that the same experience is in both so that the human heart can be fused with the natural scene until through the union the former is revealed in vivid clarity.

Thus, driven by the needs of his inner being, Lenau achieved his own individual re-creation of sky and cloud, forest and stream, mountain and steppe, as he experienced them under the changing lights and shadows of the hours, under the changing aspects of the seasons. Bright or cloudy day, dark or moonlit night, dawn or twilight become part of his unique lyric tapestry. The seasons are a central design in the pattern of his poetry; they, like the hours of the day and night, are taken to his heart and given a unique meaning as part of the personal world he created in his lyrics. Spring and autumn are the two seasons which are most important in his poetry; the former is given a special section in his collected works (ten poems); the latter, the following section of seven poems. Both seasons play a symbolic role which is central in all his lyrics. Spring is the time of love, bliss and youth; some of the few happy poems he wrote, e.g., "Festival of Love" and "Spring's Glances," are spring poems. But for Lenau, for whom melancholy is the creative mood, spring takes on a more somber significance in most of his poems: joy, love and bliss are all too brief, all too transient:

Lovely Spring, your day is done,
Nowhere, nowhere can you tarry.
—"Lament for Autumn"

Spring, by awakening the love and joy which pass so soon, only intensifies our pain. The joy of the birds and the flowers makes all the more bitter the awareness that

I only
Exiled from the spring am blighted.
—"Grief"

He has not been fated to find the joy of spring and has lost in the onrush of active life its "lovely dreams and blissful feelings" ("Too Late"). The tree that arched over him and his beloved, once more blooming richly, with its flowers he had thought came because "your joy in our love's blisses" called them forth, only serves to wake the bitterness of lost love ("The Tree of Memory"). And spring itself must die, its heart's blood pouring forth as the red roses, because

> *In Spring's full gladness our hearts felt with pain*
> *Thoughts of Lost Paradise awake and quicken.*
> *Because too loudly he had waked this pain again*
> *Pierced by sun arrows guilty Spring was stricken.*
> —*"Spring's Death"*

Summer plays a minor role in Lenau's poetry because it seems to have symbolized for him "the tense and sultry glare" of "the life of action" ("Too Late"), and was to him, therefore, usually a disturbing rather than a creative season. Nor is winter a subject treated as frequently as spring or autumn. The two poems "Winter Night" show his typical melancholy in two different aspects. In the forest, walking across the wintry land by moonlight, he sees the firs with their branches sweeping downward "as if in love with death." The quiet of the wintry landscape under the harsh cold is peaceful and contrasts with the turbulence of his own emotions until he cries:

> *Frost, freeze me to the very heart,*
> *Stilling its passion and its riot.*

In the second poem he uses the wintry scene in another way: the howling of a wolf calling its mother to feed it and the roaring winds, "mad and beyond restraining," seem so to parallel the violence of his own emotions that he tells his heart:

Let your dead come to life again
And let your sorrow's wild hordes forth
To join the storm's wild stress and strain,
Their playmate from the arctic north.

In his autumn poems he often treats winter as the final aspect of the dying year, as the symbol of life that is dead and not to be re-awakened. In "Song for Autumn" he finds the beech and not the pine close to his own heart, because the latter keeps its green in the midst of snow and ice, whereas the former tosses its last leaf on the wild wind:

More close to my heart's lamenting
Is attuned the beech tree's part,
Which takes winter's unrelenting
Pain so much to heart.

Autumn is, however, the season with which Lenau feels the deepest, the most poetically inspiring sense of kinship; poem after poem sings of the loneliness and melancholy which for him autumn symbolized. It is seldom (e.g., in "Return at Evening") that autumn is seen as the harvest time, the happy fruition of the year, a significance that its function in the economy of life makes a natural one but not for the poet who, like Lenau, has his center of creation in melancholy. For such a poet, autumn is not the culminating phase of creation but the end of life, the beginning phase of winter and death: falling leaves, bare stubble, the dying year. For him the autumn mood is that of the death of nature; the leaves flutter to earth, ever more thickly, until they hide his path

That I'd best forever stop,
Here in quiet death abiding.
—*"Autumn Mood"*

The leaves are withered and no birds sing as he takes his

lonely way; the fields lie bare of the golden grain and chill under the mist; the heart feels a longing, a homesickness, for the life that has gone; in his loneliness and in his realization that the turbulence of his heart has brought him to this lonely pain, he vows to keep his heart under harsh control

That our final journey be
Wordless wandering and lonely,
That upon our grave mound we
Have to mourn us the rain only.
—"Resolve for Autumn"

Autumn is "chill with parting's sadness"; his heart "dreams longingly of death" ("Autumn"). Autumn has left him only the "dry faggots" no life will ever quicken again; to try to kindle them to warm his heart would only "sharpen winter's woe," and so

'Twere better far and quicker
To drop them here in the snow.
—"Song of Autumn"

Autumn awakens a longing for death as the end of the heart's pain. The dead leaf that blows through his window onto the "leaves" of his false love's letters is "Death's generous word" which tells him

That every agony finds rest,
And every wound finds healing.
—"The Dead Leaf"

"The Crane" represents a somewhat atypical treatment of autumn: Lenau again sees the bare fields and leafless woods, the swirling dead leaves at his feet, the whole barren world of fall, but the call of the crane, winging surely and instinctively to a warmer and happier clime, fills his heart with the hope that he, too, like the bird of passage, will yet find "the country of his quest" where spring still awaits him. He can evoke the quiet and peace of the autumn landscape, the thatched cottage dozing, the shepherd drowsing and autumn itself in the midst of "spinning autumn hazes" falling asleep at its spinning wheel ("On a Dutch Landscape"). In the ninth "Forest Song" autumn is seen as a part of the tapestry of life in which death is only part of the design. It is seldom, however, that in his poetic treatment of autumn Lenau sees it thus as a part of the sweep of life without which life's purposes could not be accomplished. And even when he does come to such a realization, it is stated, as it were, in a minor key.

Lenau is keenly aware of the coldness, the indifference, the cruelty of nature, as it moves on its set course careless of what the human heart may be feeling. He experiences both a sense of close kinship with a kindly nature, on whose bosom he hides his face "dark with its woe" ("Melancholy"), and also a sense of its being alien and callous to human suffering. He is so sensitive to the varying aspects of nature that none of its nuances escape him. If his attitude seems paradoxical, it is the paradox of nature itself. In one mood at least, he knows that nature is cruel and without pity, that it is terrible to be dependent on "its inexorable whims"; that nature which made Sophie von Löwenthal so beautiful and entangled them in their complex relationship can, with a brief illness, snatch her away. The death of a close friend causes him to lament that nature takes away, for merely physical reasons, those on whom his heart depends, and leaves him to loneliness. The ship's boy plunges from the mast, the waves leap upon him and devour him "like hungry beasts," and then "that old murderer ocean" looks up to heaven in calm brightness as if he had done nothing ("The Ship's Boy"). We wander across the desert of life, and storms like vultures awaiting their prey wipe out our foot-prints; the sand thirsts for our "hot tears" ("In the Desert"). The tree which had once seen him and his beloved happy in their love now blooms just as richly as it did then, although his beloved has been lost to him,

For the pain when love bereft me
Is beyond your alien ken.
—"*The Tree of Memory*"

What he loved and sought is irrevocably lost; death has torn away his happiness and left no trace of it:

In nature's cruel council session
The human heart has not a place.
—"*The End*"

The ruin of the Heidelberg castle reminds him that

With indifferent grace the flowers
In bright hues and perfume play
Where o'er human graves, bright, gay,
Earth enjoys its happy hours.

He feels that the flowers are pitiless and callous to bloom gaily over the corpses of their dead sisters; but then he realizes that they are blameless because they, like the dead flowers of yesterday, are part of the irresistible surge of life toward a more complete union in death:

Nature's forces onward striving
Hasten in their endless flight;
Pity, alien, takes its flight
From the lusty callous driving.
—"*The Heidelberg Ruin*"

The wind snatches away his love's last words of farewell as he leaves her and intensifies the pain of the parting ("To the Wind"). In the two sonnets "Loneliness," the rock, the wind, the roses and even men themselves are alien and unfeeling. In an early poem the same thought appears: although happiness is gone, the earth, "faithful to its old, thoughtless habit," "still wears its roses" ("Robert and the Wounded Veteran"). In *Savonarola,* Michelangelo urges Leonardo da Vinci to leave the beautiful Medici gardens: "They seem to me so alien, so empty; the birds make me weep; the fragrance of the flowers oppresses me. Here human pain stands amid an alien art, an alien nature, cut off from their hearts, mocked by their signs of joy." In this case Christian faith is presented as the antidote to the awareness of the alien callousness of nature (and its glorification in heathen art); but this is a unique case in Lenau's poetry. In his lyrics the pain finds no such cure.

Lenau was haunted continuously by an all too vivid awareness of the transitory nature of existence, the evanescence of things physical and human, as the romantic poet so often is, seeing only "how life crumbles in time's to-and-fro" ("The Sick in Heart"). The tumultuous heart experiences the changing and not the enduring, since it measures all things by its own violent beating. The breeze blowing over the ruined castle tells Lenau that

> *All things pass and die.*

The graveyard merely bears witness that the fickle human heart cannot keep alive even its memory of the dead. Though the heart vainly tries

> *To keep its heaven in eternal holding,*

its emotions are swept away in "the mad flood" of existence; the very self changes; "the joyful tones of childhood" have

> *Died with love's magic song on some far shore;*

joy itself is fleeting; "its last tone fades and fading dies" ("Evanescence"). The tree under which he was once happy warns that

Bliss and blooming, bloom and blisses
All too quickly pass away.
—"The Tree of Memory"

He tries to retain his faith in love and happiness but the lesson the tree teaches is so obvious that his heart is filled with mourning. The distant tone of the post horn tells him that "human hearts can never stay," that "onward never ceases,"

Though the cruel lashes' crack
Tears our hearts to pieces.

The lovely night itself lasts but a moment ("The Post Horn"). Time cannot be held from its onward rush "by any human passion"; the bough sways only briefly as the raven leaves it, he tells his sorrowing love, and

Thus soon will cease the brief laments you utter.
—"Parting"

Lenau knows that

". . . To mourn what cannot tarry
Is man's autumnal fate. . . ."
—"Song of Autumn"

In an early philosophical poem, "The Skeptics," he creates an apocalyptic vision of transience: it floods all life's labyrinth, drawing all streams into its whirlpool; no dam can protect against its flood which sweeps away every living creature and overwhelms the human heart. "And if I look with trembling yearning to the stars that they may rescue my spirit, I yield to an illusion; they hear the roaring flood, they have a presentiment that they are not safe in their courses; they see the flood grow and are affrighted, as their trembling flicker tells me. Some day their shining array will sink down like weary swallows from their rapid flight." "And then over the ocean only night will brood; then death's great work will have been accomplished." At times the thought that all is transitory is a welcome one, for it means that pain and suffering are also transitory and that there is an escape from them ("The Forest Chapel"). The final release is death.

The transient nature of existence, its inability to preserve intact what is, makes Lenau's relation to the present and the past problematic. The stream of time flows on and carries away with its flood our happy youth. The innocence of childhood and youth do not last; time robs us of our youthful joys, dreams and ideals, leaving in their place disillusionment, loss of faith and guilt. The youth lingers in a flowery garden, amid roses and singing birds, happy in the dawn, a lovely expectation lighting his face; the world is heaven, man is god. "Be quiet lest you drive away the fleeting guests from him; for know that these dreams of youth are the best thing granted him in this world. But, alas, with iron stride reality approaches him, the birds fly forth forever, and the youth feels fear as he sees them take farther and farther flight" ("Youthful Dreams"). A man, lost in sadness, sees a vision of his youthful playmates in the gaiety of innocence and among them his own youthful self "with its happy mien of a stranger to earth's realm of pain"; he laments that he "trusted the sweet fairy tale of existence" and so lost his happiness. In the vision, his youthful beloved appears and again the nightingales of youth sing; but the vision fades and youth and the flowers wither; where he saw the happy vision, he now sees only the pale, bare stone ("The Rock"). The Wandering Jew laments:

Man sleeps a while within his mother's womb,
And then a while more, with his open eyes,
He dreams in hope a gay and heavenly doom,
Sleepwalking 'neath youth's airy morning skies.
Suddenly on his heart life lays its grip
And hastes his brow of his sweet dreams to strip,

With its cold hand shaking him wide awake. . . .
—"Ahasverus, the Wandering Jew"

The boy whose pet bird has flown out of its cage and is lost is warned: "Be on your guard, lest some day you stand in sorrow weeping bitterly for the loss of the best that life can give, and lay your storm-tested hand upon your breast in which so many sorrows raged and so many joys whispered, the breast from which innocence has fled in life's struggle, a timid bird" ("To a Boy"). There is no return; youth "flees and disappears deeper and deeper into the grove of the past" ("To J. Klemm"). The best man has is youth—and after that death ("Admonition"). All too often the human being is led on by hope and ambition to seek goals which are false and futile, losing the joy and innocence of youth:

That evil harlot hope once wooed me
To waste on her my early day;
I let her wanton lies delude me
And steal my young life's joys away.
—"Depression"

"Vanity" describes the "vain endeavors, empty seeking" which fill life until at its evening the futility of what the heart has sought becomes clear; the real values of life have been tossed aside, nature's offer of sanctuary—nightingales and flowers, love and friendship—has been refused. The "mad wench" ambition leads one to seek a distant goal, until, too late, one sees that

Gold or power or honor's scarlet,
Though these things she offered you,
She deceived, the lying harlot,
These are tinsel through and through.

Now as her victim stands alone by his grave, "she slips away and leaves" him; as he dies he hears only her mocking laughter from a distance. These poems represent, since Lenau did not live his life thus (he never sacrificed his ideals for glory or power, but on the contrary lived exclusively for his poetic purpose), another statement of his belief that maturity brings disillusionment and destroys youth's lovely dreams. In them man is portrayed as guilty of his own destruction and not as in other poems merely the victim of time. The latter problem is given heart-rending expression in the last poem Lenau ever wrote, "All is Vanity." Here he reaches the depths of despondency in his portrayal of the way in which man squanders his powers in seeking his varied goals. If at the achievement of the goal he were the same youth who started out so "bravely, so high-hearted," the game might be worth while. "But some power bears us onward hour by hour"; we are like a pitcher cracked against the fountain's edge

Whose water drips in slow but steady shower
Along the track until the final drop is lacking.
No water for our lips within it guarded
Among its fellow shards it falls discarded.

Lenau's belief that youth's happiness and innocence, too fragile to resist the encroaching forces of time, are destroyed by the disillusionment, pain, doubts and guilt of mature life is apparent also in his attitude toward the child:

The child's asleep. Be still! In such child faces
You can still glimpse again Lost Paradise . . .
Be silent, World, for your loud lie defaces
The truthfulness that in his sweet dreams lies.
Oh, let me hear his words—that there arise
Innocence in me that all guilt erases.

—*"Voice of the Child"*

The gay children playing around the old man seated in his garden are like happy dreams in their carefree innocence

("The Old Man"). The disillusioned knight Alfar looks back to his youth and seeks among children that which he has long ago lost, finding, burdened by guilt and fate, a brief cure with them. If some magic power could make the disillusioned and hopeless soul who is lost to honor, glory and love a child again but for an hour, could he but see the world again with a child's joyous eyes, it would give him strength to go on. But Alfar knows that the children too will soon be the victims of maturing life ("*Die Albigenser*"). There is no armor which can ward off the blows of time.

Time, as man experiences it, is not merely a linear progression from past through present to future, but rather an inextricable entanglement of past and present (and, in part, future); the past does not die with the striking of the clock but lives on in memory, casting light or shadow over the existent moment. We never live exclusively in the now but always in a confused, and for the tender-hearted, tortured fusion of the now and the then. By the sensitive Lenau, with his innate tendency to exploit all his experiences for his poetic purposes, this attribute of our experience of time is exaggerated. Memory for him becomes a vivid bliss or torture (one has to use extreme terms) which, like ghosts, haunts the house of his poetry; and forgetting becomes a release and at the same time a source of pain, since it both ends our painful memories and robs us of our happy ones. And so he prays the mist, which hides mountain, wood, river and the sun itself, to blot out the past also and take away this source of sadness ("Mist"). The problem is, however, far more complex than a mere forgetting of past sorrows. The evening star and the fragile clouds, like "a wreath of pale white roses" for the dying day, turn his thoughts to the

Graveyard of the days now sleeping,
Past, whence no word can break through.

He laments that the past, irrevocably gone from us, buries

our sorrows and dries our tears but at the same time inters our happy memories. We cannot forget the sad without also forgetting the "blisses" ("The Past"). It can, moreover, happen that the painful memory of some guilt stays vividly with us and darkens the present and perhaps all eternity ("Question"). He finds "tranquil solitude of mind" only in his sleepless hours, for in his sleep, dream a "drunken pilot" carries him either to scenes of past hate and bitterness which he would gladly forget or

To secret inlets of the past where greet us
The hopes around which youth's sweet dreams all center.
Yet what avails it? We awake—departing
Our joy is gone and our old wounds are smarting.
—*"Sleepless Night"*

Memories of past happiness are for him in his autumnal loneliness like a bundle of dry faggots, branches he had once seen filled with life and flowers; their heavy burden he must carry with him to his life's end. To rekindle these memories, as one would light a fire to warm one's self, would but prolong and intensify his pain;

'Twere better far and quicker
To drop them here in the snow.

For the sensitive heart memories cannot be cast aside until life itself ends; life continually awakens hope which is fed on lovely memories; nature would

Lure me to misery again with siren singing.

The memories of past happiness are like the brief lightning flashes across the black lake. To end the deluding sweetness of memories of past love

You must yourself seek rest, in these dark waters dying.
—*"The Dark Lake"*

The vivid awareness of being lonely which is a central

emotion in Lenau's poetry appears in some of his poems as the normal result of parting from and being kept from those he loves, as in "The Post Horn": he thinks of his distant loved ones and knows that,

Without them my life's swift flight
Passing leaves me lonely.

At times, as in "Delusion," loneliness is treated as a continuous and basic aspect of human life: he hears the owl's call, the loud storm at night, the raging winds joining in a mighty chorus, but immediately realizes that he is deluded. "All, all are lonely voices; not one knows the other." In this they are like human beings,

. . . Since our laments are monologues, unheard,
soon vanished. . . .

Earth would again be Paradise regained,

If but some day the grief that fills earth's last dimension,
Our secret sorrows, found a perfect comprehension.

But this is not the case, for what we experience in our attempt to communicate with others is only "lone, confused complaining," so that

In spite of kindly word, gesture of pity telling
Each deep pain is a lonely hermit on earth dwelling.

The two sonnets entitled "Loneliness" are Lenau's most powerful statement of the problem. The human being, bereft of God, alone, stricken by fate but too proud to complain, defying fate's further blows, with all hope lost, needs companionship so forcefully that he even embraces "the silent stone," only to start back, "frightened by loneliness," at the touch of the unfeeling rock. He turns for consolation to the wind, but it too is alien and has nothing to give. The roses, "busied with their own dying," are equally cold and unfeeling. And when the lonely seeker turns to men "they slam the windows shut before your stare"; their very abodes collapse; the lonely seeker knows only despair which

Fills the whole world and finds it cold and dead.

Faust "becomes terrifyingly aware" of being so "completely alone and cut off" that even the storm-driven waves and the lightning that zigzags across the sky seem to him to "have more of a home and a resting place than you, my lonely heart" (*Faust*). Lenau's own life was filled with a sense of loneliness; he knows only too well that he must lock his emotion "in my autumnal loneliness." Loneliness, however, has at times a more creative aspect as the source which brings him inspiration. He, therefore, drinks gladly at the forest spring of loneliness ("Loneliness"). A trip he takes to the Austrian Alps is "a pilgrimage devoted to the Madonna of Loneliness, for man the true mother of God." In a poem to Emilie Reinbeck, commemorating a walk they took together, he writes of leaving the open sunny fields (a symbol of the active life) and entering the forest, "the shadows of God's loneliness." The experience is an artistically creative and happy one ("In the Autograph Book of an Artist").

Lenau's melancholy leads him to use repeatedly the motif of Lost Paradise, to depict a realm in which the pain, the doubt, the frustration and the shortcomings of our human life do not—or did not—exist. Man has, like Adam and Eve, been driven out of Eden; he can catch glimpses of it but he can never re-enter it. Lost Paradise is for Lenau a symbol through which he can express his emotional tensions, a way of underlining by contrast the unhappy nature of human existence, a statement of an ideal condition to which life as we live it does not correspond, a glimpse of brief, bright blue seen between the storm clouds that cover his sky. The motif of Lost Paradise is born of his own experience: "I felt at the time (of his renunciation of Lotte Gmelin) as if I were cast out of Paradise forever, a Paradise which I had lost through my own fault." In explaining why he believed that a poet had by very nature to be unhappy, he told Max von Löwenthal: "the poetic organ which (the poet) possesses has a history; it belongs to another life in which alone it finds its full unfolding, hence its disharmony with our present life and the pain it feels (in its relations) with it." A troubadour moves the hearts of fair ladies so powerfully by his song that he can transport them from "the green leas of joy" to a melancholy which is in love with death, because "their hearts feel in the ecstatic song with sweet fright the breezes that once played with the golden locks of their ancestress in Eden" (*Die Albigenser*). In "The Sound of Home" he writes: every soul, as it was driven from Paradise, was given a melody before it "was wrapped in the garb of earth"; this melody still sounds in our ears, but ever less loudly. "Watch, heart, lest under the blows of suffering the last breath of this melody leave you." For Lenau poetry and its effect upon those who experience it deeply arise, in part at least, from a keen awareness of the limitations of our earthly existence as measured against the ideal of a perfect beauty, happiness and understanding, which has been lost.

Lenau's awareness that in this sense Paradise is, indeed, lost is awakened most vividly by his unhappy loves. He is like the troubadour Fulco in *Die Albigenser* whose heart was deeply moved when he looked upon his beloved, the fairest and most chaste of women, because it was as if, seeing her, he caught a glimpse—always bitter to the heart—into Lost Paradise through the iron-barred gate. In an early poem, Lenau writes: "I see your face bright in the roses' light; so once with cheeks reddened with joy man, still free from sin, saw the angel of God approach smiling in Paradise" ("Ghasel"). In the innocent sleep of a child

You still can glimpse again Lost Paradise.
—*"Voice of the Child"*

The sound of distant bells in the mountains

> *. . . recalls how peace is ever fleeing,*
> *Peace that has fled us since our day's first being,*
> *Since the first dawn of Paradise's first day. . . .*
>
> —*"Voice of the Bells"*

The nightingale is for Lenau "the songster from Eden." The effect of these glimpses into Lost Paradise upon the human heart which has been forever exiled is a source of painful longing: "He who has heard this wonderful song of home is filled with frightened homesickness and never recovers from his yearning" ("The Sound of Home").

In part the exile from Paradise is caused by forces independent of the individual, nature and the human heart casting him out of Eden in the course of their relentless activity. In "Delusion," the loneliness that makes the human heart an exile from Paradise is treated as a part of nature, the isolation of all from all; only if the world were different could we reenter Paradise. On the other hand, man's own guilt, as in *Genesis,* often causes the banishment from Paradise. Thus Lenau felt that he had exiled himself through his own guilt from the Paradise of Lotte Gmelin's love. Listening to the murmurs of the dreaming child, he cries

> *. . . Oh, let me hear his words—that there arise*
> *Innocence in me that all guilt erases. . . .*
>
> —*"Voice of the Child"*

The young man leaves the Paradise of faith, "fool that he is," to seek the Tree of Knowledge, only to find that he can never pick its golden fruit and that there is no road of return to the original state of innocence that was Eden ("Faith, Knowledge, Action").

Lenau's conception of Lost Paradise is closely enmeshed with his vision of the beauty of springtime:

In Spring's full gladness our hearts felt with pain
Thoughts of Lost Paradise awake and quicken;
Because too loudly he had waked this loss again
Pierced by sun arrows guilty Spring is stricken.
—*"Spring's Death"*

Too great natural beauty, too intense love reveal the barred gate that shuts us out of Eden; we can glimpse Lost Paradise, but not re-enter it. Though, like Don Juan, we may try "to force the firm gate of Eden and cut down the cherub at the portal," it is, indeed, a futile endeavor; the gate remains forever shut and the angel guarding it falls by no human sword.

Lenau's poetry is filled with his preoccupation with death. As he himself says of his poems, "the children of my heart talk too much of death." In a letter he writes:

> *I am not entirely well, but I am cheerful. Whether my poems are or not I do not know, but I hardly think so. A secret converse with melancholy in the lonely forests of poesie is allowed, is it not? (Gustav) Schwab is right when he accuses me of a certain monotony. I have little hope that this will change, but rather believe that the closer one attaches oneself to nature the more he is overwhelmed by its spirit of yearning, of melancholy dying.*

Death appears in many guises in Lenau's poetry, casting its varying shadow across the landscape of life as the sun of his existence follows its destined course. At first glance one might think that Lenau is merely restating the romantic attitude toward death, viz. the sense of "kinship with death" (as Thomas Mann calls it), a flight into a realm of moral irresponsibility, where, as in *Tristan und Isolde,* one escapes the demands of the "day" (moral responsibility). Death appeals to the true romantic because through it he can be free from the duties which life entails, freed of personal responsibility by the loss of personal identity. In death (and in night, too, as in Novalis and Richard Wagner) the personality and the demanding world are swallowed up in an orgiastic outburst of emotion of which death is the symbol. Lenau's attitude is different; his treatment of death is a response to his own psychological need; no mere literary influence, it wells up from the deepest springs of his nature. It is Lenau. He can treat death realistically as the bitter end of life, as the greedy devourer of that which is beautiful and loved, as in "The Three." In an early poem, written when he was ill, he says:

For me, too, the path sinks, fearful
Blows the breath of death's black deeps;
Still a youth, I yet hear, tearful,
Where the awful twilight creeps
Death's black billows flood in greeting
To my sad heart's feeble beating.
—*"In Sickness"*

He feels only too keenly that

What I have loved with deepest feeling
And sought in life is lost or dead.
Death angry tore from my possession
My happiness, nor left a trace. . . .
—*"The End"*

The shepherds in "Ahasverus, the Wandering Jew" look on the dead youth,

And all their glances cling with bitter pain
On his loved face, as if they would retain
His image in their hearts and in their eyes.

For Lenau, moreover, life and death are closely intertwined; the two of them form an indivisible whole. Looking at the stuffed vulture in his study, he realizes that "death drinks from one goblet with life"; to live the vulture must kill its prey. Both the bird striking down its prey and the plague which fills the Ganges with corpses are part of the life process; life feeds on death; the stricken prey and the floating corpses "push life forward on its path."

For Lenau death is, however, above all a release from suffering. When his pain becomes unbearable (and for the all too sensitive Lenau this point was reached quickly and experienced intensely) he sees death as the gateway of escape. He does not prefer death to life, but turns to death when the burden is too heavy. His attitude toward death is vividly evoked by his unhappy loves, especially by the frustrating affair with Sophie von Löwenthal. "Your threshold is the last at which I shall beg for anything; from it I turn to that dark threshold across which I shall step gladly or hesitating and lamenting as our love wills it." "Today I thought of death, not with bitter defiance and stubborn longing, but as desirous of grasping the hand of a good friend. This is the result of my empty life." Only seldom does he visualize a union after death: "I can long for no goal apart from you but death. And even this longing is bearable because I shall find you there and there you will not sadden me." What he wrote in these letters is put in poetic form in "Melancholy Evening":

And when I had to go, love,
And said you my last good-by,
I wished in the depths of my woe, love,
That both of us might die.

The brevity of joy, the pain of parting make his "heart dream longingly of death" ("Autumn"). Carrying a wound within him and feeling "how life crumbles in time's to-and-fro," he longs for night to still his "restless breath" and calls for his dead mother to come to "help put your weary child to bed" ("The Sick in Heart"). The dead leaf that blows through his window onto the letters his false love had written him is

> *Death's generous word, revealing*
> *That every agony finds rest*
> *And every wound finds healing.*
> —*"The Dead Leaf"*

There is consolation for the lover made mad by his sweetheart's falseness:

> *In pity whisper to him, withered leaves,*
> *This comfort: all things are transitory;*
> *And of a savior tell his soul that grieves,*
> *Of kindly death that ends the bitterest story.*
> —*"The Forest Chapel"*

The wanderer across the hot desert of life finds his futile journeying "vain and silly":

> *We move somewhere, bound together,*
> *Know not where our footsteps turn;*
> *But the sun-hot desert weather*
> *For our cool home makes us yearn.*
> —*"In the Desert"*

"Sanctuary" is a perfect statement of what death meant to Lenau: just as the child when frightened and hurt seeks refuge with its mother, so the sensitive human heart (which remains ever childlike) turns to death as a refuge, "from what pains it safely hidden." Ahasverus, the Wandering Jew, who is doomed to eternal life, expresses Lenau's own thought as he looks down on the dead shepherd boy:

> *Oh, Sleep, sweet Sleep, oh, lovely Sleep of Death,*
> *Would I could lay me in a quiet place,*
> *Could lie with him in your arms' still embrace*
> *Who knows so soon the blessing of your breath.*

I can shake off my feet the hot dust never,
Nor lie at ease in Death's sweet leisure ever,
Eyes closed that know no longer hot tears' burning,
Breast still, at rest, and free from further yearning.

Lenau's lyric genius seems to reach its finest flowering when he is singing the melancholy estate of the human heart: the transience of all things, the loneliness of human life, existence as exile from Eden, death as a release from suffering. Yet it would be false to leave the impression that, though his poetry is thus largely devoted to the shadows, it arises from a cynical or bitter condemnation of life or from a pessimistic denial of the value of life. He stresses the shadows because he loves life so much, is in love with nature and its beauty, with the entangled and entangling emotions of the human heart. The creative mind is paradox and enigma; its songs can arise from a love of light though they celebrate the shadows. This is the paradox of such a poet as Lenau: vividly as he re-creates the shadows, he does not, in so doing, overlook, deny or despise the sunlight. Without light, indeed, there can be no shadows. A very perceptive poet (who was kind enough to read and criticize these translations) stated the case clearly: "How much Lenau must have loved life to have suffered so much." There can, indeed, be no suffering like Lenau's which is not rooted in a tenacious love of life which responds to the ecstasy and bliss even when it suffers from the pain that goes hand in hand with them.

Lenau loved life, but was so constituted that he had to suffer; the suffering came in part from within himself, from his way of reacting to life. His statement of human suffering is, therefore, not an indictment of life but a revelation of the way in which the sensitive tumultuous heart experiences life. His poetry arises from certain basic attributes which shape his reaction to, and his lyric re-creation of, the external world: his vivid poetic imagination, his sensitivity and suggestibility, his rootlessness (caught between poetry and Philistine life), his tendency to overidealize reality, his consciously and unconsciously living life as a poet and his exploiting of experience for his poetic purposes. If a poet is thus constituted, he cannot but suffer, no matter how much he loves life and how gladly he would embrace it completely and joyously. Lenau reveals the nature of his situation and the basic motivation of his emphasis on death as escape in "Sanctuary":

Those whose hearts are soft and tender
From their child self ne'er have parted;
Gentler lot to them, oh, render,
Fate, than to the iron-hearted.

If misfortune's woe betide them
Seek they, by their terror ridden,
In the shroud of death to hide them,
From what pains them safely hidden.

In "Resolve for Autumn" he states the problem of the tumultuous heart:

You have many a bitter smart
To yourself and others given
By your love and hope, my heart.
That is done. We're wandering driven.

You, my heart, will be kept under
Whether gentle west winds blow
Or a tempest breaks with thunder . . .

The pain he suffers is not so much due to external forces as to his own all too violent emotions. Life can strike cruel blows as he (and every sensitive observer of life) knows; but Lenau was well aware that it was his own emotions which most frequently caused his suffering. The same thought is revealed in "The Dark Lake": the silent lake entices him to seek rest in the black water for his "heart's last wish and will" and makes him cry:

> *Down, Hopes, and down, you dreams that through my heart are weaving.*
> *Flee, Love, sweet pain of nights of sleeplessness and grieving.*

Then the storm comes and awakes his "heart to its old softness"; the rustle of the leaves is like the rustle of his beloved's dress when she once came to him; he knows, however, that the storm would only "lure (him) to misery again" and delude him into thinking that his heart can ever find what it seeks. It would be better to "seek rest, in these dark waters dying." In part the poem suggests that love and hope are themselves delusions; but in part that the blame must be put on his own heart and that, only when its tumultuousness is stilled, will he find peace. In "Winter Night I" he writes:

> *Frost, freeze me to the very heart,*
> *Stilling its passion and its riot,*
> *And to it peace at last impart*
> *As deep as this night landscape's quiet.*

In "The Dead Leaf" he describes how he feeds his own suffering consciously as he revels in the painful rereading of his false love's letters:

> *I cherish close in joyful pain*
> *What once was all my pleasure,*
> *Awake my bitter loss again*
> *By reading through my treasure.*

He knows that many of his wounds are self-inflicted and is too honest to ascribe all the guilt to the world around him. Some of his suffering comes from the nature of the world in which he lives and is objective fact; the more painful experiences, however, he owes to his own emotional make-up, his subjective reaction to what he undergoes. The shadow that lies over his life is in part the shadow he himself casts; but he is too dedicated to his poethood to wish to be otherwise than he is. After all, as we have seen, he was quite ready "to nail himself to the cross" for the sake of a poem.

To be as sensitive and as absorbed into the creative process as Lenau was deepens the shadows; it also brightens the sunlight. Lenau's poetry does both, the former more frequently than the latter. There are, however, a few poems which hymn the beauty and happiness of nature. In "Festival of Love" the larks climb the "bright ladder of their singing"; the forest, fragrant with flowers, is filled with the song of the birds; the roses burn like candles in the green candelabra of the leaves;

And every full heart pours united
To join the sacrificial stream.

In "Return at Evening" the poet, like the harvest-heavy wagons and the hunter with his full gamebag, turns homeward staggering

beneath the weight
Of thoughts and dreams immortal.

In "Springtime's Glances" the beauty of the spring—the trees waking from their winter slumber to dance green-clad in the breeze, the flowers fed with the manna of the dew, the birds breaking forth in song—is like the effect his love's glances have on him:

Thus into the wintry chill
Of my heart's deep desolation
Brought a glance so warm and still
Lovely springtime to creation.

"Safe Solitude" finds the poet and his beloved united in the quiet beauty of wood and field. The quiet ocean, and not the storm, lets his soul listen to the music of the spheres and to his own dreams "singing through its sleep," until he grasps the mystery and unity of existence ("Ocean's Silence").

In the "Forest Songs" Lenau's love of nature and of life is most beautifully revealed. Written in some of those hours when, after great emotional tension, he finds a brief moment of calm, they are a revelation of the deepest springs of Lenau's poetic genius. The emotional stress is not absent; the source of Lenau's creative activity in tension is still revealed in vivid symbols: wild storm winds like "panic breathing," the wildly flooding brook pouring through forest and across the grain fields, the thunder crashing as if the "clouds were dashed on mountain crags to pieces," the rain like his beloved's passionate weeping. The sound of the forest spring at twilight awakes memories and reminds him:

That all things die and vanish
Is an old and familiar tale;
This bitter sadness to banish
Can no man's strength avail.

Yet in spite of the turmoil and sadness in his heart there

abide
Contentment now and quiet;
My will tempered and tried
Grows strong in such hours of riot.

The forest imparts rich and full youth to those who turn to her and understand her; the heart, turning to the fountain of nature, drinks "happiness and courage." "Spirit" and "nature" are united as bride and bridegroom, as the soul is united with God, in a union so complete that it is like the surrender of death. In the fifth "Forest Song" Lenau's love for, and intimate fusion with, nature is given its most complete statement: Merlin the magician is part of nature, understanding the voice of the thunder and the lightning, the "secret springs" which send the tall oak surging toward the sky, the breathless quiet of the grass in the moonlit spring night, the sap at work in the tree trunk, the birds dreaming "tomorrow's singing." For Merlin, "the eternal poem" of nature's creativity soars up from the lowly moss itself. In the seventh "Forest Song" Lenau sings the silence of the forest, even the brooklet stilled, and praises sleep as a refuge from the day's activities and as the "way to the deepest depths" of the self, a moment of understanding as if he had heard the flute note of Pan's pipes. In the eighth, he wishes he may "part when life is over" as willingly as the birds that go to their perches to slumber after the lovely spring day of love and singing, that he may contentedly seek a sleep "more deeply stilling" than even theirs, after having once more drunk "its blisses" from the quiet fountain of love. In the last "Forest Song" autumn, which for Lenau, as we have seen, was usually a source of melancholy, has become "quiet contented change"; the birds have gone but their going is part of life's rhythm, not its end; their nests no longer "need the leaves' protecting care." Life, not "death and decay," is triumphant even in the passing of the year, even in the falling of the leaves "like amber snows"; this is the message that the gentle breeze whispers to the listening poet.

Bearing the burden of his tumultuous heart and of his dedicated poethood, Lenau lived life fully; he drank gladly at the "forest pool" of life and love, tasting their bliss as well as their pain, and never hesitated to drink deeply. Although he suffered keenly, he embraced the suffering (and the joy) and with the magic of the creative artist transformed what he suffered (and enjoyed) into melodious verse. In spite of its tendency to focus on the shadows of human existence (to the point, as he himself puts it, of "monotony") his poetry is not that of a victim of life, crushed by its burden, but that of a strong man who, turning his burden into a source of creativity, achieved his life's purpose before his tragic breakdown overwhelmed him.

SELECTED POEMS

VERGÄNGLICHKEIT

Vom Berge schaut hinaus ins tiefe Schweigen
Der mondbeseelten schönen Sommernacht
Die Burgruine; und in Tannenzweigen
Hinseufzt ein Lüftchen, das allein bewacht
Die trümmervolle Einsamkeit,
Den bangen Laut: "Vergänglichkeit!"

"Vergänglichkeit!" mahnt mich im stillen Tale
Die ernste Schar bekreuzter Hügel dort,
Wo dauernder der Schmerz in Totenmale
Als in verlaßne Herzen sich gebohrt;
Bei Sterbetages Wiederkehr
Befeuchtet sich kein Auge mehr.

Der wechselnden Gefühle Traumgestalten
Durchrauschen äffend unser Herz; es sucht
Vergebens seinen Himmel festzuhalten,
Und fortgerissen in die rasche Flucht
Wird auch der Jammer; und der Hauch
Der sanften Wehmut schwindet auch.

Horch' ich hinab in meines Busens Tiefen,
"Vergänglichkeit!" klagt's hier auch meinem Ohr,
Wo längst der Kindheit Freudenkläng' entschliefen,
Der Liebe Zauberlied sich still verlor;
Wo bald in jenen Seufzer bang
Hinstirbt der letzte frohe Klang.

EVANESCENCE

The ruined castle on the mountain gazes
Across the silence of the summer night
Beneath the moon's spell; and a light breeze raises,
Sole guardian of the loneliness, in flight
Amid the pines a low sad sigh
And tells us: "All things pass and die."

That all things pass and die the somber crosses
In yon still valley on the graves repeat,
Where gravestones hold in memory our losses
More lastingly than fickle hearts' swift beat;
When comes again the day they died
We face its dawning light dry-eyed.

Emotions' dreams in changing forms unfolding
Pour mocking through our heart which vainly tries
To keep its heaven in eternal holding;
Carried away in the mad flood there flies
Our sorrow too; and too the breath
Of gentle sadness flies in death.

And if I listen to my inner being,
That all things pass and die I hear once more;
For there the joyful tones of childhood fleeing
Died with love's magic song on some far shore;
For there amid our frightened sighs
Joy's last tone fades and fading dies.

DAS DÜRRE BLATT

Durchs Fenster kommt ein dürres Blatt,
Von Wind hereingetrieben;
Dies leichte, offne Brieflein hat
Der Tod an mich geschrieben.

Das dürre Blatt bewahr' ich mir,
Will's in die Blätter breiten,
Die ich empfangen einst von ihr;
Es waren schöne Zeiten!

Da draußen steht der Baum so leer;
Wie er sein Blatt im Fluge,
Kennt sie vielleicht ihr Blatt nicht mehr,
Trotz ihrem Namenszuge.

Der toten Liebe Worte flehn,
Daß ich auch sie vernichte;
Wie festgehaltne Lügner stehn
Sie mir im Angesichte.

Doch will ich nicht dem holden Wahn
Den Wurf ins Feuer gönnen;
Die Worte sehn mich traurig an,
Daß sie nicht sterben können.

Ich halte fest, zu bittrer Lust,
Was all mein Glück gewesen,
In meinen schmerzlichen Verlust
Will ich zurück mich lesen.

Das dürre Blatt leg' ich dazu,
Des Todes milde Kunde,
Daß jedes Leiden findet Ruh',
Und Heilung jede Wunde.

THE DEAD LEAF

A dead leaf through my window blew
And on my table lighted,
A light and open billet-doux
To me by death indited.

I'll keep the dead leaf safe and well
Between the written pages
Which once from her to my lot fell
In far and happier ages.

Outside the tree stands bare and spent;
It knows its leaf no better
Than she perhaps the leaf she sent,
Although she signed her letter.

The words of love now dead demand
That I destroy their treasure;
Like liars caught in lies they stand
Before my face's displeasure.

But I'll not grant the sweet lies' will,
The hypocrites, and burn them;
They look so sad, and yet I still
Ensure that death shall spurn them.

I cherish close in joyful pain
What once was all my pleasure,
Awake my bitter loss again
By reading through my treasure.

The dead leaf with these leaves be pressed,
Death's generous word, revealing
That every agony finds rest
And every wound finds healing.

NEBEL

Du trüber Nebel, hüllest mir
Das Tal mit seinem Fluß,
Den Berg mit seinem Waldrevier
Und jeden Sonnengruß.

Nimm fort in deine graue Nacht
Die Erde weit und breit!
Nimm fort, was mich so traurig macht,
Auch die Vergangenheit!

MIST

Before my eyes, sad Mist, you veil
The mountain and the wood,
The river flowing through the dale,
The sun's beatitude.

Take from me with your night's pale gray
The whole world, far and wide,
What makes me sad, oh, take away,
The Past, the Yestertide.

UNMUT

Die Hoffnung, eine arge Dirne,
Verbuhlte mir den Augenblick,
Bestahl mit frecher Lügenstirne
Mein junges Leben um sein Glück.

Nun ist's vorüber; in den Tagen,
Als ihr Betrug ins Herz mir schnitt,
Hab' ich das süße Kind erschlagen,
Und mit dem Leben bin ich quitt.

Nicht mehr zum Lustschloß umgelogen,
Scheint mir die Erde, was sie ist:
Ein schwankes Zelt, das wir bezogen
—Tod, habe Dank!—auf kurze Frist.

Zu lange doch dünkt mir das Brüten
Hier unter diesem schwanken Zelt!
Ergreif es, Sturm, mit deinem Wüten,
Und streu' die Lappen in die Welt!

DEPRESSION

That evil harlot Hope once wooed me
To waste on her my early day;
I let her wanton lies delude me
And steal my young life's joy away.

But now it's over; in my passion,
When her deceit my poor heart tore,
I slew my sweet in lover's fashion:
Now life and I have even score.

My Spanish castles all dispelling,
I see my life now clear and true,
A flimsy tent for hasty dwelling—
Thanks be to Death—an hour or two.

Too long I find this brooding under
The flimsy tent where I abide;
Storm, seize it with your raging thunder
And strew the tatters far and wide.

VERGANGENHEIT

Hesperus, der blasse Funken,
Blinkt und winkt uns traurig zu.
Wieder ist ein Tag gesunken
In die stille Todesruh;

Leichte Abendwölkchen schweben
Hin im sanften Mondenglanz,
Und aus bleichen Rosen weben
Sie dem toten Tag den Kranz.

Friedhof der entschlafnen Tage,
Schweigende Vergangenheit!
Du begräbst des Herzens Klage,
Ach, und seine Seligkeit!

THE PAST

Hesperus, a pale spark shining,
Sends sad greetings from the west,
And another day declining
Enters into death's still rest.

Fragile evening cloud reposes
Where the moon's soft light is shed,
Like a wreath of pale white roses
For the day that now is dead.

Graveyard of the days now sleeping,
Past, whence no word can break through,
You inter the heart's sore weeping
And, alas, its blisses, too.

HERBSTLIED

Rings trauern die Entlaubten,
Vom kalten Wind durchweht,
Die Tannen nur behaupten
Ihr dunkles Grün so spät.

Wenn's Vöglein baut sein Lager,
So grünt das Tannenreis,
Und grünt, wenn's Wild sich hager
Scharrt Wurzeln aus dem Eis.

Die Buche seh' ich schwinden
Im Froste, lebenssatt,
Wie sie den kalten Winden
Hinwirft das letzte Blatt.

Zu meiner Seele Trauer
Die Buche besser stimmt,
Daß sie den Winterschauer
Sich so zu Herzen nimmt.

SONG FOR AUTUMN

Around me sorrow leafless
The trees in the fall wind's chill;
The pines alone are griefless,
Keeping their dark green still.

In spring when birds are nesting,
Then green the pine trees show,
And green when the deer go questing
For food to dig from the snow.

I watch the beech tree wither
Weary of life in the frost,
To the cold wind's hither and thither
Its final leaf is tossed.

More close to my heart's lamenting
Is attuned the beech tree's part,
Which takes winter's unrelenting
Pain so much to heart.

AN DIE MELANCHOLIE

Du geleitest mich durchs Leben,
Sinnende Melancholie!
Mag mein Stern sich strahlend heben,
Mag er sinken—weichest nie!

Führst mich oft in Felsenklüfte,
Wo der Adler einsam haust,
Tannen starren in die Lüfte,
Und der Waldstrom donnernd braust.

Meiner Toten dann gedenk' ich,
Wild hervor die Träne bricht
Und an deinen Busen senk' ich
Mein umnachtet Angesicht.

TO MELANCHOLY

Through my life you are attendant,
Melancholy, everywhere;
Be my star bright and ascendant,
Be it sinking, you are there.

Oft you lead to precipices
Where the eagle nests alone,
Where the stream down sheer abysses
Through the stunted pines is thrown.

Mem'ries of my dead awaking
Wake my tears to wildly flow;
Refuge on your bosom taking
Rests my face dark with its woe.

ZUFLUCHT

Tut man Kindern was zuleide,
Fliehn zur Mutter sie voll Schrecken,
Sich in ihrem Faltenkleide
Vor dem Quäler zu verstecken.

Weiche Herzen bleiben Kinder
All ihr Leben, und es falle
Ihnen auch das Los gelinder
Als den Herzen von Metalle.

Jagt sie Unglück, wie zum Fluche,
Fliehn sie bang und immer bänger,
Bis sie hinterm Leichentuche
Sich verbergen ihrem Dränger.

SANCTUARY

Hurt, a child seeks sanctuary
With its mother, terror-ridden,
In her skirts its face to bury,
From what hurts it safely hidden.

Those whose hearts are soft and tender
From their child-self ne'er have parted;
Gentler lot to them, oh render,
Fate, than to the iron-hearted.

If misfortune's woe betide them
Seek they, by their terror ridden,
In the shroud of death to hide them,
From what pains them safely hidden.

HIMMELSTRAUER

Am Himmelsantlitz wandelt ein Gedanke,
Die düstre Wolke dort, so bang, so schwer;
Wie auf dem Lager sich der Seelenkranke,
Wirft sich der Strauch im Winde hin und her.

Vom Himmel tönt ein schwermutmattes Grollen,
Die dunkle Wimper blinzet manchesmal,
—So blinzen Augen, wenn sie weinen wollen,—
Und aus der Wimper zuckt ein schwacher Strahl.

Nun schleichen aus dem Moore kühle Schauer
Und leise Nebel übers Heideland;
Der Himmel ließ, nachsinnend seiner Trauer,
Die Sonne lässig fallen aus der Hand.

HEAVEN'S MOURNING

Athwart the brow of heaven a thought is crossing,
Yon somber cloud heavy and full of woe;
Like someone sick at heart upon his pallet tossing,
The bushes in the wind toss to and fro.

The sky is rent with melancholy sighing,
Its somber lashes move a time or two,
Like eyes upon the verge of bitter crying—
And from them pale light weakly flashes through.

Across the moors chill mists rise up and thicken,
And chill mists sink upon the heather land;
The heaven, by its bitter sorrow stricken,
Let weary fall the sun from out its hand.

HERBSTGEFÜHL

Mürrisch braust der Eichenwald,
Aller Himmel ist umzogen,
Und dem Wandrer, rauh und kalt,
Kommt der Herbstwind nachgeflogen.

Wie der Wind zu Herbsteszeit
Mordend hinsaust in den Wäldern,
Weht mir die Vergangenheit
Von des Glückes Stoppelfeldern.

An den Bäumen, welk und matt,
Schwebt des Laubes letzte Neige,
Niedertaumelt Blatt auf Blatt
Und verhüllt die Waldessteige;

Immer dichter fällt es, will
Mir den Reisepfad verderben,
Daß ich lieber halte still,
Gleich am Orte hier zu sterben.

AUTUMN MOOD

Angrily the oak trees scold,
Overhead the clouds are racing,
And the fall wind, harsh and cold,
On the wanderer's track is chasing.

When the winds of autumn blow
And their blasts the forests trouble,
Blows the past, the long-ago,
From my joy's bare fields of stubble.

On the trees now tired and dead
Still a few last leaves are clinging;
Leaf by leaf they're slowly shed,
Slowly to the pathway winging.

Ever thicker the leaves drop,
Ever more my pathway hiding,
That I'd best forever stop,
Here in quiet death abiding.

HERBSTKLAGE

Holder Lenz, du bist dahin!
Nirgends, nirgends darfst du bleiben!
Wo ich sah dein frohes Blühn,
Braust des Herbstes banges Treiben.

Wie der Wind so traurig fuhr
Durch den Strauch, als ob er weine;
Sterbeseufzer der Natur
Schauern durch die welken Haine.

Wieder ist, wie bald! wie bald!
Mir ein Jahr dahingeschwunden.
Fragend rauscht es aus dem Wald:
"Hat dein Herz sein Glück gefunden?"

Waldesrauschen, wunderbar
Hast du mir das Herz getroffen!
Treulich bringt ein jedes Jahr
Welkes Laub und welkes Hoffen.

LAMENT FOR AUTUMN

Lovely Spring, your day is done,
Nowhere, nowhere can you tarry.
Where I saw your flowers and sun
Autumn winds now hunt and harry.

Sadly sighs fall's fading breath
Through the leafless branches tearful;
Nature breathes her last in death;
Fading flowers shudder fearful.

Once again how fleetingly
Has a year slipped through my fingers;
Fading forests question me:
"Have you found the joy that lingers?"

Wake the answer my heart's sought
With the question they sent thither:
Faithfully each year has brought
Withered leaves and hopes that wither.

BITTE

Weil' auf mir, du dunkles Auge,
Übe deine ganze Macht,
Ernste, milde, träumerische,
Unergründlich süße Nacht!

Nimm mit deinem Zauberdunkel
Diese Welt von hinnen mir,
Daß du über meinem Leben
Einsam schwebest für and für.

PRAYER

Rest upon me, dark eyes, bind me
With your darkly magic might,
Earnest, mild, and deeply dreaming,
Inexplicably sweet Night.

With your magic darkness rid me
Of the world of garish day,
That you over my life ever,
You alone, hold perfect sway.

LIEBESFEIER

An ihren bunten Liedern klettert
Die Lerche selig in die Luft;
Ein Jubelchor von Sängern schmettert
Im Walde voller Blüt' und Duft.

Da sind, so weit die Blicke gleiten,
Altäre festlich aufgebaut,
Und all die tausend Herzen läuten
Zur Liebesfeier dringend laut.

Der Lenz hat Rosen angezündet
An Leuchtern von Smaragd im Dom;
Und jede Seele schwillt und mündet
Hinüber in den Opferstrom.

FESTIVAL OF LOVE

High up bright ladders of their singing
The larks climb gaily to the skies;
A choir of jubilation's ringing
In forests where flower perfumes rise.

On every side our glances fleeting
See festive altars now arrayed;
By every heart with joyful beating
The call to worshipping is made.

In green-leaf holders spring has lighted
Rose-candles till its shrine's agleam,
And every full heart pours united
To join the sacrificial stream.

WINTERNACHT

I

Vor Kälte ist die Luft erstarrt,
Es kracht der Schnee von meinen Tritten,
Es dampft mein Hauch, es klirrt mein Bart;
Nur fort, nur immer fortgeschritten!

Wie feierlich die Gegend schweigt!
Der Mond bescheint die alten Fichten,
Die, sehnsuchtsvoll zum Tod geneigt,
Den Zweig zurück zur Erde richten.

Frost! friere mir ins Herz hinein,
Tief in das heißbewegte, wilde!
Daß einmal Ruh mag drinnen sein,
Wie hier im nächtlichen Gefilde!

II

Dort heult im tiefen Waldesraum
Ein Wolf;—wie's Kind aufweckt die Mutter,
Schreit er die Nacht aus ihrem Traum
Und heischt von ihr sein blutig Futter.

Nun brausen über Schnee und Eis
Die Winde fort mit tollem Jagen,
Als wollten sie sich rennen heiß;
Wach' auf, o Herz, zu wildem Klagen!

Laß deine Toten auferstehn,
Und deiner Qualen dunkle Horden!
Und laß sie mit den Stürmen gehn,
Dem rauhen Spielgesind aus Norden!

WINTER NIGHT

I

With cold the air is still as death,
Beneath my feet the snow cracks brittle;
My beard is iced, white hangs my breath;
Onward, stride on, nor pause a little.

How solemn-still the landscape lies,
The moon on the old firs is shining;
As if in love with death they rise,
Their branches back to earth inclining.

Frost, freeze me to the very heart,
Stilling its passion and its riot,
And to it peace at last impart
As deep as this night landscape's quiet.

II

A wolf howls in the forest's chill,
A child that calls its mother, waking
The night from sleep to come and still
Its hunger with a bloody taking.

Now roar across the ice and snow
The winds, mad and beyond restraining;
As if to warm themselves they blow.
Wake up, my heart, to wild complaining!

Let your dead come to life again
And let your sorrow's dark hordes forth
To join the storm's wild stress and strain,
Their playmate from the arctic north.

DIE SCHILFLIEDER

I

Drüben geht die Sonne scheiden,
Und der müde Tag entschlief.
Niederhangen hier die Weiden
In den Teich, so still, so tief.

Und ich muß mein Liebstes meiden:
Quill, o Träne, quill hervor!
Traurig säuseln hier die Weiden,
Und im Winde bebt das Rohr.

In mein stilles, tiefes Leiden
Strahlst du, Ferne! hell und mild,
Wie durch Binsen hier und Weiden
Strahlt des Abendsternes Bild.

II

Trübe wird's, die Wolken jagen,
Und der Regen niederbricht,
Und die lauten Winde klagen:
"Teich, wo ist dein Sternenlicht?"

Suchen den erloschnen Schimmer
Tief im aufgewühlten See.
Deine Liebe lächelt nimmer
Nieder in mein tiefes Weh!

SEDGE SONGS

I

The sun sinks beyond the sedges,
Weary day now falls asleep,
Drooping willows touch the edges
Of the lake, so still, so deep.

From my dearest love I'm parted;
Tears, my tears, pour forth and flow!
Willows rustle, sad, down-hearted;
Sedges quake as the winds blow.

Through the sorrows that confound me
Your love, Sweet, shines from afar,
As through sedge and willow round me
Shines the lovely evening star.

II

Through the dull skies clouds are flying,
On the earth the wild rains break;
Winds in loud lament are crying:
"Where is now your starlight, lake?"

What they ask is quenched forever
In the waters' storm-tossed flow;
Your love smiles upon me never,
Never smiles on my deep woe.

III

Auf geheimem Waldespfade
Schleich' ich gern im Abendschein
An das öde Schilfgestade,
Mädchen, und gedenke dein!

Wenn sich dann der Busch verdüstert,
Rauscht das Rohr geheimnisvoll,
Und es klaget und es flüstert,
Daß ich weinen, weinen soll.

Und ich mein', ich höre wehen
Leise deiner Stimme Klang,
Und im Weiher untergehen
Deinen lieblichen Gesang.

IV

Sonnenuntergang;
Schwarze Wolken ziehn,
O wie schwül und bang
Alle Winde fliehn!

Durch den Himmel wild
Jagen Blitze, bleich;
Ihr vergänglich Bild
Wandelt durch den Teich.

Wie gewitterklar
Mein' ich dich zu sehn
Und dein langes Haar
Frei im Sturme wehn!

III

Sweet at sunset time to wander
Where a hidden path slips through
To the sedge-lined bayside yonder,
To my memories of you.

Twilight shrouds the trees in sadness,
Through the reeds mysterious go
Whispers that lament lost gladness,
Till my own tears start to flow.

And I think I hear the sighing
Of your voice sound soft and low,
Hear your lovely song, dear, dying,
Lost in the dark waters' flow.

IV

Sunset, end of day,
Black clouds cross the sky;
Heavy with dismay
Sultry winds now fly.

Through the startled skies
Lightning flickers stark,
Fleeting mirrored lies
In the waters' dark.

Clear I see you there
As the lightning glows;
Loosened, free, your hair
In the wild wind blows.

V

Auf dem Teich, dem regungslosen,
Weilt des Mondes holder Glanz,
Flechtend seine bleichen Rosen
In des Schilfes grünen Kranz.

Hirsche wandeln dort am Hügel,
Blicken in die Nacht empor;
Manchmal regt sich das Geflügel
Träumerisch im tiefen Rohr.

Weinend muß mein Blick sich senken,
Durch die tiefste Seele geht
Mir ein süßes Deingedenken,
Wie ein stilles Nachtgebet.

V

Motionless the lake reposes
Silvered by the moonlight's sheen,
Moonlight weaves its silver roses
In the sedges' wreath of green.

On the hillside deer are straying,
Look up at the nightime sky;
In the sedge the lake birds swaying,
Dreaming on the water lie.

Quick tears rise and blind my seeing,
In my deepest heart abide
Thoughts of you that fill my being
Like a prayer at eventide.

FRÜHLINGS TOD

Warum, o Lüfte, flüstert ihr so bang?
Durch alle Haine weht die Trauerkunde,
Und störrisch klagt der trüben Welle Gang:
Das ist des holden Frühlings Todesstunde!

Der Himmel, finster und gewitterschwül,
Umhüllt sich tief, daß er sein Leid verhehle,
Und an des Lenzes grünem Sterbepfühl
Weint noch sein Kind, sein liebstes, Philomele.

Wenn so der Lenz frohlocket, schmerzlich ahnt
Das Herz sein Paradies, das uns verloren,
Und weil er uns zu laut daran gemahnt,
Mußt' ihn der heiße Sonnenpfeil durchbohren.

Der Himmel blitzt und Donnerwolken fliehn,
Die lauten Stürme durch die Haine tosen;
Doch lächelnd stirbt der holde Lenz dahin,
Sein Herzblut still verströmend, seine Rosen.

SPRING'S DEATH

Why, breezes, do you whisper thus in woe?
Through all the woodlands the sad news is sighing,
And there is bitter mourning in the waters' flow,
For Spring, for lovely Spring, this hour is dying.

The sky, darkened and sultry with the storm,
To hide its grief its face in clouds is veiling,
And by Spring's deathbed that the green leaves form
His dearest child, the nightingale, is wailing.

In Spring's full gladness our hearts felt with pain
Thoughts of Lost Paradise awake and quicken:
Because too loudly he had waked this loss again,
Pierced by sun arrows guilty Spring was stricken.

The flashes fill the sky, the storm cloud flies,
The loud storms through the woods are screaming;
But smiling gently lovely Springtime dies;
The roses, his heart's blood, are softly streaming.

AHASVER, DER EWIGE JUDE

Ein Wäldchen rauscht auf weiter grüner Heide;
Hier lebt die Erde still und arm und trübe;
Das Wäldchen ist ihr einziges Geschmeide,
Daran ihr Herz noch hangen mag in Liebe,
Wie eine Witwe, eine einsam arme,
Den Brautschmuck aufbewahrt, daß sie die Blicke,
Die tränenvollen, spät daran erquicke,
Wird sie zu bang erfaßt von ihrem Harme.
Rings um das Wäldchen alles öd' und einsam;
Nicht Baum und Strauch, nur Wiesengrund zu sehn
Bis an die Grenze, wo die Wolken gehn,
Wo Heid' und Himmel zweifelnd wird gemeinsam.
Strohhütten stehn umher zerstreut im Haine;
Hier hat ein traulich stilles Los gefunden
Von Hirten eine friedliche Gemeine;
Doch ist kein Menschenleben ohne Wunden.
Die Linde säuselt, blütenreich und hoch,
Die Sonne geht im Westen still verloren,
Und auf den Blüten, die sie jüngst geboren,
Verweilen ihre warmen Blicke noch;
Auch strahlen sie zum letztenmal auf einen,
Um dessen Leiche dort die Hirten weinen.
Sie stellten seine Bahre an die Linde,
Als sollt' ihn einmal noch der Lenz begrüßen,
Der schon als Jüngling hat hinsterben müssen.
Die bleiche Mutter kniet an ihrem Kinde;
Mit Rosenkränzen schmücken ihn Jungfrauen,
Und aller Blicke haften schmerzumflossen
Auf ihrem lieben, freundlichen Genossen,
Sein Bild sich recht ins treue Herz zu schauen.
Der Vater hält des Toten Flöt' und Stab,
Benetzend sie mit mancher heißen Zähre;

AHASVERUS, THE WANDERING JEW

A small wood rustles mid a wide green plain;
Here earth lives quietly and meagerly;
This copse is her sole jewel, her heart is fain
To pour on it her full love eagerly,
A widow who now living poor and lonely
Treasures her bridal jewels and seeks relief
In looking on them when her bitter grief
Waxes too strong, and there finds solace only.
Beyond the wood is silence; none lives there;
No tree nor bush, but meadow-land is green
To the horizon where far clouds are seen
And heath and sky commingle earth and air.
Straw huts are scattered in a little wood,
And here a shepherd's quiet community
Has found a fate, simple and still and good;
Yet without wound no human life can be.
The flowering linden whispers from its height,
The west'ring sun is almost lost to earth,
Yet on the blossoms that her rays gave birth
Her warm glance lingers still with gentle light;
And too her rays for the last time are stealing
Across a dead face, where the shepherds kneeling
Weep by a bier placed by the flowery tree
As if spring should give him her final greeting
Who, still a youth, has found life quickly fleeting.
Pale kneels the mother by him, wreaths of roses
Each maiden lays beside him as he lies,
And all their glances cling with bitter pain
On his loved face, as if they would retain
His image in their hearts and in their eyes.
His father holds the dead son's flute and crook,
On which his ever-flowing tears are falling;

Dem Jüngling sollen folgen in sein Grab
Die schlichten Zeichen seiner Hirtenehre.
Im Ohr des Alten summen noch die Lieder,
Die dieser Flöte einst so froh entquollen,
Und die auf immer nun ihm schweigen sollen;
Das beugt ihm tiefer noch die Seele nieder.—

Wer aber kommt die Heide hergezogen,
Gejagt, so scheint's, von drängender Gewalt,
Das Haupt von greisen Locken wild umflogen,
Das tiefgefurchte Antlitz fahl und kalt?
Es ragt ins Leben ernst und schroff herein
Wie altes, längst verwittertes Gestein;
Vom Antlitz fließt herab der Bart so hell,
Wie düsterm Fels entstürzt der Silberquell.
Aus dunkler Höhle glüht des Auges Stern,
Als säh's auf dieser Erde nichts mehr gern.
Das Auge scheint mit seiner Glut zu sagen:
"Müßt' ich nicht leuchten dem unsteten Fuß,
Ich hätte längst mit eklem Überdruß
Vor dieser Welt die Türe zugeschlagen!"
Der Wandrer ist der Jude Ahasver,
Der, fluchgetrieben, rastlos irrt umher.
Zur Bahre tritt er feierlich und leise,
Und spricht im bang erschrocknen Hirtenkreise:
"So! betet still, daß ihr ihn nicht erweckt!
Hemmt eurer Tränen undankbare Flut!
Sein Schlaf ist gut, o dieser Schlaf ist gut!
Wenn er auch Toren euresgleichen schreckt.
O süßer Schlaf! o süßer Todesschlaf!
Könnt' ich mich rastend in die Grube schmiegen!
Könnt' ich, wie d e r, in deinen Armen liegen,
Den schon so früh dein milder Segen traf!
Den Staub nicht schütteln mehr vom müden Fuße!
Wie tief behaglich ist die Todesmuße!

In death he shall take, as in life he took,
These simple symbols of his shepherd's calling.
Still in his father's ears the songs are ringing
Which his son's flute but lately loved to trill
And now are silenced and forever still,
His bowed head nearer to his last sleep bringing.

But who is this that now the steppe is crossing,
By some wild driving urge, it seems, controlled,
Around his head wildly his gray locks tossing,
His furrowed face both pale and cold?
In life's warm midst it seems to stand alone,
As juts a rigid and age-weathered stone;
And from the face the gray beard downward sweeps
As from dark crags a silver torrent leaps;
From their dark caves his eyes burn glowingly
As though they wearied of the world they see;
Their fiery glances seem like words to pour:
"Were we not bound to light these restless feet,
With satiation and disgust replete,
We should upon the world have slammed our door."
The stranger is the Wandering Jew whose feet
Curse-driven walk the whole world's restless street.
Solemnly, softly, he steps to the bier
And speaks; his words the frightened shepherds hear:
"Pray quietly, lest you should wake him dead,
And check your flowing tears' ingratitude.
His sleep is good, I say, this sleep is good,
Though to such fools as you it may seem dread.
Oh Sleep, sweet Sleep, oh lovely Sleep of Death,
Would I could lay me in so quiet a place,
Could lie, like him, in your arms' still embrace
Who knows so soon the blessings of your breath.
I can shake off my feet the hot dust never,
Nor lie at ease in Death's sweet leisure ever,

Das Auge ist verschlossen, ohne Tränen;
Die Brust so still, so flach und ohne Sehnen;
Die Lippen bleich, versunken, ohne Klage,
Verschwunden von der Stirn die bange Frage.
Wohl ihm! er starb in seinen Jugendtagen;
Er hat gar leicht, vom Schicksal liebgewonnen,
Die große Schuld des Schmerzes abgetragen,
Das Leben ihm umsonst Verrat gesponnen.
Sein Herz ist still; das meine, ohne Rast,
Pocht Tag und Nacht in ungeduld'ger Hast,
Auf daß es einmal endlich fertig werde
Und seinen Sabbat find' in kühler Erde.
Es schläft der Mensch in seiner Mutter Hüften,
Dann eine Weile noch, mit Augen offen,
Irrt er, Schlafwandler, in den Morgenlüften
Und träumt ein buntes, himmlisch frohes Hoffen,
Bis plötzlich ihm ans Herz das Leben greift,
Den schönen Traum von trunkner Stirne streift,
Und ihn mit kalter Hand ins Wachen schüttelt,
Wie meine Hand hier Blüten niederrüttelt.
D e n hat die kalte Faust noch nicht erfaßt,
Er ist, unaufgeschreckt vom Traum, erblaßt;
Ich seh's an seinen ruhig schönen Zügen,
Die, selig lächelnd, fast den Tod verhehlen,
Und immer noch das Märchen still erzählen,
Die Erde noch zum Paradiese lügen!"
Er rüttelt wieder Blüten von den Zweigen,
Die niederflattern ihren Todesreigen:
"Noch immer, Erde, den uralten Tand
Von Blütentreiben und Zerstören, immer?
Verdrießt, Natur, das öde Spiel dich nimmer?
Ergreift nicht Schläfrigkeit die müde Hand?
Du gleichest mit dem wüsten Zeitvertreib
Im Dorfe drüben dem Zigeunerweib,
Die Karten schlägt, mit ihren bunten Bildern

Eyes closed that know no longer hot tears' burning,
Breast still, at rest, and free from further yearning,
Lips pale and sunken, done with all complaining,
The brow with questioning and with explaining.
It's well with him; he dies in youth's sweet days;
And without any smart, fate's favored son,
Pain's heavy debt he meets and lightly pays.
For him life treacherous webs has vainly spun;
His heart is still; but mine can never wait,
But beats by day and night importunate
To speed the moment of its final stay
And in the cool earth find its Seventh Day.
Man sleeps awhile within his mother's womb
And then awhile more, with his open eyes,
He dreams in hope a gay and heavenly doom,
Sleepwalking neath youth's airy morning skies;
Suddenly on his heart life lays its grip
And hastes his brow of his sweet dreams to strip,
With its cold hand shaking him wide awake,
As from this branch these blossoms now I shake.
But him this cold hand did not frighten thus;
His dream still undisturbed, he went from us.
I see it in his peaceful features plainly;
His sweet smile almost hides that here death lies
And seems to prove the dream men hold insanely:
That earth can ever be a paradise."
He shakes again the branch, white petals fly
And float down, in their dance of death, to die.
"What, Earth, this age-old farce, this empty play,
Of flowering and destruction holds you ever?
This empty farce revolts you, Nature, never?
Does drowsiness not bid your hand to stay?
This silly game to fill your empty years
Is like yon village gipsy's, who appears
By laying cards and reading from their faces

Vergangnes wie Zukünftiges zu schildern,
Und, blöd begafft, belauscht, neugierigen Leuten,
Was sie gedacht, was sie geträumt, zu deuten.
Die Blätter werden aufgemengt und frisch
Gelegt in neuer Ordnung auf den Tisch,
Den Glauben äffend mit prophet'schen Spuren;
Doch immer sind's die nämlichen Figuren!
Ich schaute zu seit achtzehnhundert Jahren,
Die machtlos über mich dahingefahren.—
Laß dich umarmen, Tod, in dieser Leiche!
Mein Auge laben an der Wangen Bleiche!
Balsamisch rieselt ihre frische Kühle
Durch mein Gebein, durch meines Hirnes Schwüle."—
Derweil die Hirten jetzt den Sarg verschließen,
Starrt Ahasver aufs Kruzifix der Decke,
Als ob er plötzlich, tiefgemahnt, erschrecke,
Aus seinem finstern Auge Tränen fließen:
"Hier ist sein Bildnis an den Sarg geheftet,
Der einst gekommen, schmachtend und entkräftet,
Der einst vor meiner Tür zusammenbrach,
Gebeugt vom Druck des Kreuzes und der Schmach,
Der mich um kurze Rast so bang beschwor;
Ich aber stieß ihn fort, verfluchter Tor!
Nun bin auch ich vom Fluche fortgestoßen,
Und alle Gräber sind vor mir verschlossen.
Ich stand, ein Bettler, weinend vor der Türe
Der Elemente, flehte um den Tod;
Doch, ob ich auch den Hals mit Stricken schnüre,
Mein fester Leib erträgt des Odems Not.
Das Feuer und die Flut, die todesreichen,
Versagten das ersehnte Todesglück;
Ich sah die scheue Flamme rückwärts weichen,
Mit Ekel spie die Welle mich zurück.
War ich geklettert auf die Felsenmauer,
Wo nichts gedeiht als süßer Todesschauer,

To tell what time will bring, what time has brought,
And for the silly curious gapers places
Interpretation on their dream and thought.
Ever the cards are shuffled, new deals made,
That, in new combinations on the table laid,
They may mock faith and seem to prophesy;
Always the same card faces fall and lie.
I've watched for eighteen hundred years, not feeling
Time's power, which cannot bring me death or healing.
Let me embrace you, Death, in him who lies
Here dead, and on his pale cheeks feast my eyes.
Like balsam on my forehead falls death's chill,
Touching my fevered limbs till pain is still."
Now while the shepherds close the coffin lid
The wanderer on the cross has fixed his eyes;
It seems that sudden memories, long hid
Deep in his soul, with bursting tears arise.
"This crucifix portrays the One who came
Once worn and weary like a burnt out flame,
Bowed by the cross and by his weight of shame,
On me in pain for a brief respite calling;
Fool that I was, I drove him from my door.

Now by the curse I'm driven evermore
And find that every grave is locked and barred.
I've stood, a beggar, before Nature's portal
Pleading for death to free from life immortal;
Yet, though I sought relief by deadly cord
My body breathed and would not let me free;
Nor fire nor flood obeyed their usual lord
And granted death's joy as a boon to me.
I saw the shy flame frightened backward shrinking;
With horror saw the billow cast me back;
And, though I climbed the dizzy rock where thinking
Turned to sweet horror and naught lived but fear,

Und rief ich weinend, wütend abgrundwärts:
“O Mutter Erde, dein verlorner Sohn!
Reiß mich zerschmetternd an dein steinern Herz!”
Der Zug der Erdentiefe sprach mir Hohn,
Sanft senkten mich die fluchgestärkten Lüfte,
Und lebend, rasend, irrt’ ich durch die Klüfte.
“Tod!” rief ich, “Tod!”, mich in die Erde krallend,
“Tod!” höhnte Klipp’ an Klippe widerhallend.
Zu Bette stieg ich lüstern mit der Pest;
Ich habe sie umsonst ans Herz gepreßt.
Der Tod, der in des Tigers Rachen glüht,
Der zierlich in der gift’gen Pflanze blüht,
Der schlängelnd auf dem Waldespfade kriecht,
Den Wandrer lauernd in die Ferse sticht,
Mich nahm er nicht!”—
Da wandte sich der Jude von den Hirten,
Und weiter zog der Wandrer ohne Ruh,
Dem letzten Strahl der Abendsonne zu;
Ob seinem Haupt die Heidevögel schwirrten.
Und wie er fortschritt auf den öden Matten,
Zog weithingreifend sich sein Schattenstrich
Bis zu den Hirten; die bekreuzten sich,
Die Weiber schauderten an seinem Schatten.

And called in tears and rage on Earth to hear:
"Oh Earth, my mother, I, your lost son, call,
Grant me the bliss on your stone heart to fall!"
The pull of Earth's depths failed and mocking o'er me
The curse-strong air safely and gently bore me.
And living, raging, I strayed through abysses.
"Death," cried I, "Death!" and clutched the earth in madness;
"Death" mocked the echoes from the precipices.
I lay with Pestilence in wild embrace
In vain—death was not in my pulses' race.
Nor death that in the tiger's red mouth glows,
And in some lovely poison blossom blows,
Or creeps, a serpent, on the forest floor
To strike the wanderer's heel with venom hot,
They freed me not."
Then the Jew turned and left the herdsmen, bent
His step upon his ever restless quest,
Toward sunset light fast fading in the west;
Above his head the steppe birds circling went.
And as he strode across the desert meadow
His lengthening shadow on the herdsmen fell;
They crossed themselves against its somber spell;
The women shuddered at the long, dark shadow.

DER POSTILLION

Lieblich war die Maiennacht,
Silberwölklein flogen,
Ob der holden Frühlingspracht
Freudig hingezogen.

Schlummernd lagen Wies' und Hain,
Jeder Pfad verlassen;
Niemand als der Mondenschein
Wachte auf der Straßen.

Leise nur das Lüftchen sprach,
Und es zog gelinder
Durch das stille Schlafgemach
All der Frühlingskinder.

Heimlich nur das Bächlein schlich,
Denn der Blüten Träume
Dufteten gar wonniglich
Durch die stillen Räume.

Rauher war mein Postillion,
Ließ die Geißel knallen,
Über Berg und Tal davon
Frisch sein Horn erschallen.

Und von flinken Rossen vier
Scholl der Hufe Schlagen,
Die durchs blühende Revier
Trabten mit Behagen.

Wald und Flur im schnellen Zug
Kaum gegrüßt—gemieden;
Und vorbei, wie Traumesflug,
Schwand der Dörfer Frieden.

THE POSTILLION

Lovely was the night in May;
Silver clouds were flying
Over springtime's fair array
Far beneath them lying.

Sleeping lay both field and wood,
Lonely every byway;
No one but the moonlight stood
Watch upon the highway.

Only breezes spoke, and they
Tiptoe-still went creeping
Through the chamber where there lay
Springtime's children sleeping.

Secretly the brook slipped on,
Deep the perfumes breathing
That the flowers' dreams had thrown
Through the still night wreathing.

My postillion was less still;
Cracks his long whip's lashes;
Gaily over vale and hill
Bugle notes he flashes.

The four horses swiftly stride,
And with loud hoofs beating
Through the lovely countryside
Cheerily are fleeting.

Wood and field in rapid flight,
Hardly greeted, vanished.
And our speeding through the night
Dreamlike hamlets banished.

Mitten in dem Maienglück
Lag ein Kirchhof innen,
Der den raschen Wanderblick
Hielt zu ernstem Sinnen.

Hingelehnt an Bergesrand
War die bleiche Mauer,
Und das Kreuzbild Gottes stand
Hoch, in stummer Trauer.

Schwager ritt auf seiner Bahn
Stiller jetzt und trüber;
Und die Rosse hielt er an,
Sah zum Kreuz hinüber:

"Halten muß hier Roß und Rad!
Mag's euch nicht gefährden:
Drüben liegt mein Kamerad
In der kühlen Erden!

Ein gar herzlieber Gesell!
Herr, 's ist ewig schade!
Keiner blies das Horn so hell,
Wie mein Kamerade!

Hier ich immer halten muß,
Dem dort unterm Rasen
Zum getreuen Brudergruß
Sein Leiblied zu blasen!"

Und dem Kirchhof sandt' er zu
Frohe Wandersänge,
Daß es in die Grabesruh'
Seinem Bruder dränge.

Suddenly a churchyard lay
Dark amid May's gladness,
Brought the wanderer on his way
Heavy thoughts and sadness.

Nestled to the mountainside
Lay the pale wall, by it
Stood the cross and Crucified
Sorrowful and quiet.

Now more sadly, now more still
Went my driver, turning
At the cross upon the hill
Glances full of yearning.

"Here must halt both horse and wheel—
Do not be astounded;
Yonder lies my comrade leal
Where the cool earth's mounded.

"He was aye a comrade dear;
What a shame he's left me.
None could blow a horn as clear—
Death has sore bereft me.

"I must always linger here,
To blow in loving greeting
To my sleeping comrade cheer,
Songs he loved repeating."

Wander-melodies he blew
Which had pleased the other
That they pierce the grave's peace through
To his sleeping brother.

Und des Hornes heller Ton
Klang vom Berge wider,
Ob der tote Postillion
Stimmt' in seine Lieder.—

Weiter ging's durch Feld und Hag
Mit verhängtem Zügel;
Lang mir noch im Ohre lag
Jener Klang vom Hügel.

When the bugle's echo rang
From the mountain clearly,
'Twas as if the sleeper sang
Songs he'd once loved dearly.

Onward then past field and fen,
Riverside and rillside,
Hearing ever and again
Yon echo from the hillside.

TRAUER

Blumen, Vögel, duftend, singend,
Seid doch nicht so ausgelassen,
Ungestüm ans Herz mir dringend;
Laßt allein mich ziehn die Straßen!

Vieles ist vorübergangen,
Seit wir uns zuletzt begegnet,
Und es hat von meinen Wangen
Meines Glückes Herbst geregnet.

Winter kam hereingeschlichen
In mein Herz, die Tränen starben,
Und schneeweiß sind mir verblichen
Alle grünen Hoffnungsfarben.

Blumen, Vögel, rings im Haine,
All' ihr frohen Bundsgenossen,
Mahnt mich nicht, daß ich alleine
Bin vom Frühling ausgeschlossen!

GRIEF

Singing bird and fragrant flower,
Need your joy burst in such riot,
Storm my heart with such wild power?
Let me go my way in quiet.

From how many things we've parted
Since last time we came together;
And my tears have often started
In my joy's autumnal weather.

Winter stealthily came o'er me,
Chilled my heart and stilled my weeping;
And I saw hope's green before me
Pale to white in his fell keeping.

Birds and flowers, never lonely,
But in common joy united,
Don't remind me that I only
Exiled from the spring am blighted.

AUS!

Ob jeder Freude seh' ich schweben
Den Geier bald, der sie bedroht;
Was ich geliebt, gesucht im Leben,
Es ist verloren oder tot.

Fort riß der Tod in seinem Grimme
Von meinem Glück die letzte Spur;
Das Menschenherz hat keine Stimme
Im finstern Rate der Natur.

Ich will nicht länger töricht haschen
Nach trüber Fluten hellem Schaum,
Hab' aus den Augen mir gewaschen
Mit Tränen scharf den letzten Traum.

THE END

Above each joy my eyes see wheeling
A vulture threatening overhead.
What I have loved with deepest feeling
And sought in life is lost or dead.

Death, angry, tore from my possession
My happiness, nor left a trace;
In nature's cruel council session
The human heart has not a place.

No more my foolish hands try keeping
The bright foam on life's somber stream;
And from my eyes with bitter weeping
I've washed away my final dream.

HERBSTENTSCHLUSS

Trübe Wolken, Herbstesluft,
Einsam wandl' ich meine Straßen,
Welkes Laub, kein Vogel ruft—
Ach, wie stille! wie verlassen!

Todeskühl der Winter naht;
Wo sind, Wälder, eure Wonnen?
Fluren, eurer vollen Saat
Goldne Wellen sind verronnen!

Es ist worden kühl und spät,
Nebel auf der Wiese weidet,
Durch die öden Haine weht
Heimweh;—alles flieht und scheidet.

Herz, vernimmst du diesen Klang
Von den felsentstürzten Bächen?
Zeit gewesen wär' es lang,
Daß wir ernsthaft uns besprechen!

Herz, du hast dir selber oft
Wehgetan, und hast es andern,
Weil du hast geliebt, gehofft;
Nun ist's aus, wir müssen wandern!

Auf die Reise will ich fest
Ein dich schließen und verwahren,
Draußen mag ein linder West
Oder Sturm vorüberfahren;

Daß wir unsern letzten Gang
Schweigsam wandeln und alleine,
Daß auf unsern Grabeshang
Niemand als der Regen weine!

RESOLVE FOR AUTUMN

Heavy clouds and breath of fall;
Lonely I my way have taken;
Withered leaves, and no birds' call:
Ah, how silent, how forsaken!

Cold as death the winter nears;
Where, oh forest, are your blisses?
Fields, your waves of golden ears
In their ebb our sad eye misses.

Cool the day attains its close;
Mist now floats upon the meadows;
Homesickness the night wind blows;
All flees, leaving us like shadows.

Heart, can you now hear the song
Of the brooklet pouring hither?
You and I should have, how long,
Earnestly conversed together.

You have many a bitter smart
To yourself and others given
By your love or hope, my heart.
That is done. We're wandering driven.

On the journey we now go,
You, my heart, will be kept under,
Whether gentle west winds blow
Or a tempest breaks with thunder,

That our final journey be
Wordless wandering and lonely,
That upon our grave-mound we
Have to mourn us the rain only.

SCHLAFLOSE NACHT

Schlaflose Nacht, du bist allein die Zeit
Der ungestörten Einsamkeit!
Denn seine Herde treibt der laute Tag
In unsern grünenden Gedankenhag,
Die schönsten Blüten werden abgefressen,
Zertreten oft im Keime und vergessen.
Trägt aber uns der Schlaf mit weicher Hand
Ins Zauberboot, das heimlich stößt vom Strand
Und lenkt das Boot im weiten Ozean
Der Traum herum, ein trunkner Steuermann,
So sind wir nicht allein, denn bald gesellen
Die Launen uns der unbeherrschten Wellen
Mit Menschen mancherlei, vielleicht mit solchen,
Die feindlich unser Innres tief verletzt,
Bei deren Anblick sich das Herz entsetzt,
Getroffen von des Hasses kalten Dolchen;
An denen gerne wir vorüberdenken,
Um tiefer nicht den Dolch ins Herz zu senken.—
Dann wieder bringen uns die Wellenfluchten,
Wohin wir wachend nimmermehr gelangen,
In der Vergangenheit geheimste Buchten,
Wo uns der Jugend Hoffnungen empfangen.
Was aber hilft's? wir wachen auf—entschwunden
Ist all das Glück, es schmerzen alte Wunden.
Schlaflose Nacht, du bist allein die Zeit
Der ungestörten Einsamkeit!

SLEEPLESS NIGHT

Oh, Sleepless Night, your hours alone I find
Give tranquil solitude of mind.
For ever raucous day his flocks has brought
To graze the fertile meadows of our thought,
The fairest blossoms greedily are eaten,
Forgotten buds fall by their hoofs down beaten.
And when Sleep bears us with its gentle hand
Into his magic boat, and from the strand
Dream, drunken pilot, steers mysteriously,
Then we are not alone, for soon surround us,
Fantastic, born of the wild waves around us,
A varied host; and in the cavalcade
Those who as foes have hurt our deepest heart,
Whose sight with utter horror makes us start,
Stricken as by hate's cold steel dagger blade,
Those whom our thoughts would gladly pass unseeing,
The deeper thrust of that fell dagger fleeing.
Or, yet again, the unruled billows beat us
Whither awake we cannot ever enter,
To secret inlets of the past where greet us
The hopes round which our youth's sweet dreams all center—
Yet what avails it? We awake—departing
Our joy is gone, and our old wounds are smarting.
Oh, Sleepless Night, your hours alone I find
Give tranquil solitude of mind.

DER SEELENKRANKE

Ich trag' im Herzen eine tiefe Wunde,
Und will sie stumm bis an mein Ende tragen;
Ich fühl' ihr rastlos immer tiefres Nagen,
Und wie das Leben bricht von Stund' zu Stunde.

Nur eine weiß ich, der ich meine Kunde
Vertrauen möchte und ihr alles sagen;
Könnt' ich an ihrem Halse schluchzen, klagen!
Die eine aber liegt verscharrt im Grunde.

O Mutter, komm, laß dich mein Flehn bewegen!
Wenn deine Liebe noch im Tode wacht,
Und wenn du darfst, wie einst, dein Kind noch pflegen,

So laß mich bald aus diesem Leben scheiden,
Ich sehne mich nach einer stillen Nacht,
O hilf dem Schmerz dein müdes Kind entkleiden!

THE SICK IN HEART

Deep in my heart a mortal wound I know;
Silent I'll bear it till life's utter end;
I feel its restless fangs that deeper rend
And how life crumbles in time's to-and-fro.

To one alone I would lament my woe;
To her alone my inmost sorrow send
Its cry of pain; and to her bosom bend
My heavy head—but she died long ago.

O, Mother, come, nor heedless, hear my prayer.
If your dear love wakes still in very death,
And if you may, as once, give me your care,

Soon from this life let my last step be sped;
I wish still night to still my restless breath,
Oh, help pain put your weary child to bed.

HERBSTLIED

Ja, ja, ihr lauten Raben
Hoch in der kühlen Luft,
's geht wieder ans Begraben,
Ihr flattert um die Gruft!

Die Wälder sind gestorben,
Hier, dort ein leeres Nest;
Die Wiesen sind verdorben;
O kurzes Freudenfest!

Ich wandre hin und stiere
In diese trübe Ruh',
Ich bin allein und friere,
Und hör' euch Raben zu.

Auch mir ist Herbst, und leiser
Trag' ich den Berg hinab
Mein Bündel dürre Reiser,
Die mir das Leben gab.

Einst sah ich Blüten prangen
An meinem Reiserbund,
Und schöne Lieder klangen
Im Laub, das fiel zu Grund.

Die Bürde muß ich tragen
Zum letzten Augenblick;
Den Freuden nachzuklagen,
Ist herbstliches Geschick.

SONG OF AUTUMN

Aye, you loud ravens flying
In air that's chill with doom,
Again it's time for dying;
You flutter round the tomb.

The forest's done with living;
Bare nests show here and yon;
The fields have naught for giving;
How quick joy's feast sped on.

Onward I stride and ponder
And see the sad peace lie;
Chilly, alone I wander
And hear you ravens cry.

Me, too, has autumn stricken,
And soft to my shoulder I lift
These faggots life cannot quicken,
To me its only gift.

I once saw flowers springing
From these branches dry and dead;
I once heard lovely singing
In these leaves whose life is fled.

This burden I must carry
To where my last hours wait;
To mourn that joy cannot tarry
Is man's autumnal fate.

Soll mit dem Rest ich geizen,
Und mit dem Reisig froh
Mir meinen Winter heizen?
Ihr Raben, meint ihr so?

Erinnerungen schärfen
Mir nur des Winters Weh;
Ich möchte lieber werfen
Mein Bündel in den Schnee.

With life shall I be a miser?
To light with these twigs a glow
To warm my winter were wiser?
You ravens, do you think so?

These mem'ries would only flicker
To sharpen winter's woe.
'Twere better far and quicker
To drop them here in the snow.

DER SCHWERE ABEND

Die dunklen Wolken hingen
Herab so bang und schwer,
Wir beide traurig gingen
Im Garten hin und her.

So heiß und stumm, so trübe
Und sternlos war die Nacht,
So ganz wie unsre Liebe
Zu Tränen nur gemacht.

Und als ich mußte scheiden
Und gute Nacht dir bot,
Wünscht' ich bekümmert beiden
Im Herzen uns den Tod.

MELANCHOLY EVENING

The dark clouds, tense and fearful,
Hung earthward dull and low;
We two were walking tearful
In the garden to and fro.

Somber the sky above, dear,
Nor star through the hot air shone,
A symbol of our love, dear,
Created for tears alone.

And when I had to go, love,
And said you my last good-by,
I wished in the depths of my woe, love,
That both of us might die.

AN DIE ENTFERNTE

I

Diese Rose pflück' ich hier,
In der fremden Ferne;
Liebes Mädchen, dir, ach dir
Brächt' ich sie so gerne!

Doch bis ich zu dir mag ziehn
Viele weite Meilen,
Ist die Rose längst dahin,
Denn die Rosen eilen.

Nie soll weiter sich ins Land
Lieb' von Liebe wagen,
Als sich blühend in der Hand
Läßt die Rose tragen;

Oder als die Nachtigall
Halme bringt zum Neste,
Oder als ihr süßer Schall
Wandert mit dem Weste.

II

Rosen fliehen nicht allein,
Und die Lenzgesänge,
Auch dein Wangenrosenschein,
Deine süßen Klänge.

O, daß ich, ein Tor, ein Tor,
Meinen Himmel räumte!
Daß ich einen Blick verlor,
Einen Hauch versäumte!

TO MY FARAWAY BELOVED

I

This rose that I'm plucking here,
In an alien land, love,
I would gladly bring my dear,
Lay it in your hand, love.

E'er I conquered time and tide,
Miles and miles that waste, love,
Would these roses long have died;
Roses have to haste, love.

Never farther from its home
Should love leave its land, love,
Than a living rose can roam
In a lover's hand, love.

Than the nightingale can bring
Straws to build its nest, love,
Or as far as its notes ring
When the wind is west, love.

II

More than roses waste and fail,
More than springtime joys, love;
Soon your rosy cheek will pale,
Soon grow still your voice, love.

What a wretched fool I've been
To depart from you, love,
Leave a single glance unseen,
Lose a whisper, too, love.

Rosen wecken Sehnsucht hier,
Dort die Nachtigallen,
Mädchen, und ich möchte dir
In die Arme fallen!

Nightingales and roses, too,
Tell us love is best, love;
And my heart would haste to you,
In your arms to rest, love.

TRAURIGE WEGE

Bin mit dir im Wald gegangen;
Ach, wie war der Wald so froh!
Alles grün, die Vögel sangen,
Und das scheue Wild entfloh.

Wo die Liebe frei und offen
Rings von allen Zweigen schallt,
Ging die Liebe ohne Hoffen
Traurig durch den grünen Wald.—

Bin mit dir am Fluß gefahren;
Ach, wie war die Nacht so mild!
Auf der Flut, der sanften, klaren,
Wiegte sich des Mondes Bild.

Lustig scherzten die Gesellen;
Unsre Liebe schwieg und sann,
Wie mit jedem Schlag der Wellen
Zeit und Glück vorüberrann.—

Graue Wolken niederhingen,
Durch die Kreuze strich der West,
Als wir einst am Kirchhof gingen;
Ach, wie schliefen sie so fest!

An den Kreuzen, an den Steinen
Fand die Liebe keinen Halt;
Sahen uns die Toten weinen,
Als wir dort vorbeigewallt?

MELANCHOLY PATHS

Once in the forest we walked together,
Ah, the forest was then so gay;
All was green, and 'twas singing weather;
Shyly the wild deer fled away.

There where love was freely spoken,
Sweetly sung from every spray,
Our love walked with hopes all broken
Sadly along our woodland way.

Once our boat on the river drifted,
Ah, the night was then so sweet;
Clearly and gently sank and lifted
The mirrored moon on the ripples' beat.

Gaily rippled the bright waves' laughter,
Our love spoke not, knowing well
Time and joy ran ever after
The fleeting water's whispered spell.

Gray the sky and stormy the weather;
Through the crosses the west wind wept,
As we walked by the graves together;
Ah, how soundly the dead all slept.

Cross nor stone which the gray sky covers
Offered our love a place to stay.
Did the dead behold us lovers
Weeping sore as we passed that way?

STIMME DES KINDES

Ein schlafend Kind! o still! in diesen Zügen
Könnt ihr das Paradies zurückbeschwören;
Es lächelt süß, als lauscht' es Engelchören,
Den Mund umsäuselt himmlisches Vergnügen.

O schweige, Welt, mit deinen lauten Lügen
Die Wahrheit dieses Traumes nicht zu stören!
Laß mich das Kind im Traume sprechen hören,
Und mich, vergessend, in die Unschuld fügen!

Das Kind, nicht ahnend mein bewegtes Lauschen,
Mit dunklen Lauten hat mein Herz gesegnet,
Mehr als im stillen Wald des Baumes Rauschen;

Ein tiefres Heimweh hat mich überfallen,
Als wenn es auf die stille Heide regnet,
Wenn im Gebirg' die fernen Glocken hallen.

VOICE OF THE CHILD

The child's asleep. Be still! In such child faces
You can still glimpse again Lost Paradise;
He smiles—at voices out of heavenly skies
And lovely melodies of heavenly places.

Be silent, World, for your loud lie defaces
The truthfulness that in his sweet dreams lies.
Oh, let me hear his words that there arise
Innocence in me that all guilt erases.

He knows not how I listen, moved, to him;
Mysterious tones have blessed my heart again
More deep than sound of trees in forest dim;

A deeper homesickness my heart now fills
Than ever on the steppes in quiet rain,
Than ever when bells call across far hills.

EINSAMKEIT

I

Hast du schon je dich ganz allein gefunden,
Lieblos und ohne Gott auf einer Heide,
Die Wunden schnöden Mißgeschicks verbunden
Mit stolzer Stille, zornig dumpfem Leide?

War jede frohe Hoffnung dir entschwunden,
Wie einem Jäger an der Bergesscheide
Stirbt das Gebell von den verlornen Hunden,
Wie's Vöglein zieht, daß es den Winter meide?

Warst du auf einer Heide so allein,
So weißt du auch, wie's einen dann bezwingt,
Daß er umarmend stürzt an einen Stein;

Daß er, von seiner Einsamkeit erschreckt,
Entsetzt empor vom starren Felsen springt
Und bang dem Winde nach die Arme streckt.

II

Der Wind ist fremd, du kannst ihn nicht umfassen,
Der Stein ist tot, du wirst beim kalten, derben
Umsonst um eine Trosteskunde werben,
So fühlst du auch bei Rosen dich verlassen;

Bald siehst du sie, dein ungewahr, erblassen,
Beschäftigt nur mit ihrem eignen Sterben.
Geh weiter: überall grüßt dich Verderben
In der Geschöpfe langen, dunklen Gassen;

LONELINESS

I

If ever you have found yourself alone,
Loveless, bereft of God, upon the plain,
And bound your wounds, silent, too proud to groan,
Defying fate to strike you once again;

If ever every happy hope has flown,
As listens to his lost pack's cry in vain
The mountain hunter and hears how far their tone,
As flees the bird from winter's snow and rain;

Were you thus on a lone heath all alone,
You know then too how some force made you kneel
And fling your arms around a silent stone;

And how, frightened by loneliness, you rise
In horror from the rock that cannot feel
And stretch your arms out to the windy skies.

II

The wind is alien; your arms naught enfold;
The stone is dead; from it you seek in vain
A word of comfort that might still your pain;
The gentle roses are no whit less cold;

You see them, unaware of you, unfold—
Busied with their own dying; and again
Where'er you turn decay and death obtain
And all life's highways in their thralldom hold.

Siehst hier und dort sie aus den Hütten schauen,
Dann schlagen sie vor dir die Fenster zu,
Die Hütten stürzen, und du fühlst ein Grauen.

Lieblos und ohne Gott! der Weg ist schaurig,
Der Zugwind in den Gassen kalt; und du?—
Die ganze Welt ist zum Verzweifeln traurig.

And if you see from out their huts men start
They slam the windows shut before your stare;
The huts collapse; stark horror grips your heart.

Loveless, bereft of God, your path is dread;
The wind of life grows cold; your own despair
Fills the whole world and finds it cold and dead.

FRÜHLINGSGRÜSSE

Nach langem Frost, wie weht die Luft so lind!
Da bringt Frühveilchen mir ein bettelnd Kind.

Es ist betrübt, daß so den ersten Gruß
Des Frühlings mir das Elend bringen muß.

Und doch der schönen Tage liebes Pfand
Ist mir noch werter aus des Unglücks Hand.

So bringt dem Nachgeschlechte unser Leid
Die Frühlingsgrüße einer bessern Zeit.

SPRING GREETING

After long cold, the air blows warm and mild;
First violets brings to me a beggar child.

I find it sad that spring's first greeting be
Brought to me in the hand of misery.

And yet this pledge of fairer days to be
From sadness' hand is dearer still to me.

So to posterity our present sorrow
Brings the spring greeting of a better morrow.

DIE DREI ZIGEUNER

Drei Zigeuner fand ich einmal
Liegen an einer Weide,
Als mein Fuhrwerk mit müder Qual
Schlich durch sandige Heide.

Hielt der eine für sich allein
In den Händen die Fiedel,
Spielte, umglüht vom Abendschein,
Sich ein feuriges Liedel.

Hielt der zweite die Pfeif' im Mund,
Blickte nach seinem Rauche,
Froh, als ob er vom Erdenrund
Nichts zum Glücke mehr brauche.

Und der dritte behaglich schlief,
Und sein Cimbal am Baum hing,
Über die Saiten der Windhauch lief,
Über sein Herz ein Traum ging.

An den Kleidern trugen die drei
Löcher und bunte Flicken,
Aber sie boten trotzig frei
Spott den Erdengeschicken.

Dreifach haben sie mir gezeigt,
Wenn das Leben uns nachtet,
Wie man's verraucht, verschläft, vergeigt,
Und es dreimal verachtet.

Nach den Zigeunern lang noch schaun
Mußt' ich im Weiterfahren,
Nach den Gesichtern dunkelbraun,
Den schwarzlockigen Haaren.

THE THREE GYPSIES

Once three gypsies I chanced to find
Camped by a willow together
As my carriage with lurch and grind
Toiled through the sand and the heather.

The one of them sat with his fiddle alone
And played with flying fingers
A little song with fire in its tone
In the light where the sunset lingers.

The second sat, pipe in his mouth,
And only its smoke he heeded,
As if on earth, north, west, east, south,
Nothing else for joy was needed.

In perfect comfort the third man slept;
On a tree his zither apart swings;
Over its strings the wind's breath crept
And a dream over his heartstrings.

On their clothes they wore, these three,
Rags in every condition;
But none the less defiantly free
They bade fate go to perdition.

In a threefold fashion the three of them say:
When life is melancholy,
Just smoke, or sleep, or fiddle it away
And thrice despise its folly.

To the gypsies long my eyes turned back
While my carriage onward paces,
Back to the locks of curly black,
Back to the swarthy faces.

DER KRANICH

Stoppelfeld, die Wälder leer,
Und es irrt der Wind verlassen,
Weil kein Laub zu finden mehr,
Rauschend seinen Gruß zu fassen.

Kranich scheidet von der Flur,
Von der kühlen, lebensmüden,
Freudig ruft er's, daß die Spur
Er gefunden nach dem Süden.

Mitten durch den Herbstesfrost
Schickt der Lenz aus fernen Landen
Dem Zugvogel seinen Trost,
Heimlich mit ihm einverstanden.

O wie mag dem Vogel sein,
Wenn ihm durch das Nebeldüster
Zückt ins Herz der warme Schein,
Und das ferne Waldgeflüster!

Hoch im Fluge übers Meer
Stärket ihn der Duft der Auen;
O wie süß empfindet er
Ahnung, Sehnsucht und Vertrauen!

Nebel auf die Stoppeln taut;
Dürr der Wald;—ich duld' es gerne,
Seit gegeben seinen Laut
Kranich, wandernd in die Ferne.

Hab' ich gleich, als ich so sacht
Durch die Stoppeln hingeschritten,
Aller Sensen auch gedacht,
Die ins Leben mir geschnitten;

THE CRANE

Stubble fields and woods lie bare,
And the sad wind strays forsaken
By the leaves that everywhere
Rustled by his greetings shaken.

From the lifeless, icy ground
Now the crane his way is speeding;
Gay his cry proclaims he's found
Sky-born pathways southward leading.

Through the heart of autumn's chill
Spring has sent the bird of passage
Secret comfort and the thrill
Of a far, compulsive message.

Ah, what joy the bird must know
When through fogs and cold mists wreathing
Warm he feels the sun, below
Hears the southern forests' breathing.

High in flight above the sea
Fragrant distant meadows lure him;
Prescience, yearning, faith—these three
Ever sweetly reassure him.

Mist upon the stubble's wet;
Dead the woods. I do not mind it,
Since my ears are hearing yet
Cries his far flight left behind it.

Though I pondered as I went,
Through the stubble slowly straying,
How life's scythe had cut and rent
Deep my life, my joys low-laying;

Hab' ich gleich am dürren Strauch
Andres Welk bedauern müssen
Als das Laub, vom Windeshauch
Aufgewirbelt mir zu Füßen:

Aber ohne Gram und Groll
Blick' ich nach den Freudengrüften,
Denn das Herz im Busen scholl,
Wie der Vogel in den Lüften;

Ja, das Herz in meiner Brust
Ist dem Kranich gleich geartet,
Und ihm ist das Land bewußt,
Wo mein Frühling mich erwartet.

Though my bitter tears have wept
Other fading than the dying
Withered leaves the wind has swept
Round my feet in whirlpools flying;

Still I mourn not, nor complain
Though I see my joy's graves lying;
For my heart has leaped again
Like the crane above me flying.

Aye, the heart within my breast
Like the crane feels what elates me,
Knows the country of my quest
Where my springtime still awaits me.

KOMMEN UND SCHEIDEN

So oft sie kam, erschien mir die Gestalt
So lieblich, wie das erste Grün im Wald.

Und was sie sprach, drang mir zum Herzen ein
Süß, wie des Frühlings erstes Lied im Hain.

Und als Lebwohl sie winkte mit der Hand,
War's, ob der letzte Jugendtraum mir schwand.

COMING AND PARTING

Whene'er she came her being seemed to me
As lovely as the first green on the tree.

And when she spoke my heart was sweetly stirred
As by spring's first song in a forest heard.

And when her hand waved me her last good-by,
It was as if I saw youth's last dream die.

AUF EINE HOLLÄNDISCHE LANDSCHAFT

Müde schleichen hier die Bäche,
Nicht ein Lüftchen hörst du wallen,
Die entfärbten Blätter fallen
Still zu Grund, vor Altersschwäche.

Krähen, kaum die Schwingen regend,
Streichen langsam; dort am Hügel
Läßt die Windmühl' ruhn die Flügel;
Ach, wie schläfrig ist die Gegend!

Lenz und Sommer sind verflogen;
Dort das Hüttlein, ob es trutze,
Blickt nicht aus, die Strohkapuze
Tief ins Aug' herabgezogen.

Schlummernd, oder träge sinnend,
Ruht der Hirt bei seinen Schafen,
Die Natur, Herbstnebel spinnend,
Scheint am Rocken eingeschlafen.

ON A DUTCH LANDSCAPE

Here the very streams are weary;
Not a sound the breezes utter;
To the earth the still leaves flutter,
Tired with age and drab and dreary.

Crows on barely moving pinion
Slowly fly, and on that hilltop
Lets the mill its sail arms still stop.
Ah, how slumbrous this dominion.

Spring has fled and summer's fleeing,
Yonder cottage as if sulky
Draws down on its eyes its bulky
Straw-thatch cap and lolls unseeing.

Slumb'ring or with daydreams dowered
Near his flock the shepherd lazes;
Nature, spinning autumn hazes,
At her wheel sleep's overpowered.

DIE DREI

Drei Reiter nach verlorner Schlacht,
Wie reiten sie so sacht, so sacht!

Aus tiefen Wunden quillt das Blut,
Es spürt das Roß die warme Flut.

Vom Sattel tropft das Blut, vom Zaum,
Und spült hinunter Staub und Schaum.

Die Rosse schreiten sanft und weich,
Sonst flöss' das Blut zu rasch, zu reich.

Die Reiter reiten dicht gesellt,
Und einer sich am andern hält.

Sie sehn sich traurig ins Gesicht,
Und einer um den andern spricht:

"Mir blüht daheim die schönste Maid,
Drum tut mein früher Tod mir leid."

"Hab' Haus und Hof und grünen Wald,
Und sterben muß ich hier so bald!"

"Den Blick hab' ich in Gottes Welt,
Sonst nichts, doch schwer mir's Sterben fällt."

Und lauernd auf den Todesritt
Ziehn durch die Luft drei Geier mit.

Sie teilen kreischend unter sich:
"Den speisest du, den du, den ich."

THE THREE

From a battle lost come riders three;
How gentle, how gentle the ride must be.

From mortal wounds pours down the blood,
The horses feel the warm red flood.

From saddle, from bridle the blood drops spray,
Washing the foam and dust away.

The steeds stride gently, soft and slow,
Else would the blood too richly flow.

Close pressed together, side by side,
They seek support as they slowly ride.

Sad they look in each other's eyes
And each to the other whispering sighs:

"I have the fairest bride at home,
And so unwelcome death will come."

"House, hearth and forest green have I,
And yet here shortly must I die!"

"Just eyes to see God's world have I,
That's all; and yet it's hard to die."

Awaiting the end of the ride of death
Three vultures fly, and with greedy breath

They share their prey and screaming cry:
"Him you devour, him you, him I."

DER LENZ

Da kommt der Lenz, der schöne Junge,
Den alles lieben muß,
Herein mit einem Freudensprunge
Und lächelt seinen Gruß;

Und schickt sich gleich mit frohem Necken
Zu all den Streichen an,
Die er auch sonst dem alten Recken,
Dem Winter, angetan.

Er gibt sie frei, die Bächlein alle,
Wie auch der Alte schilt,
Die der in seiner Eisesfalle
So streng gefangen hielt.

Schon ziehn die Wellen flink von dannen
Mit Tänzen und Geschwätz
Und spötteln über des Tyrannen
Zerronnenes Gesetz.

Den Jüngling freut es, wie die raschen
Hinlärmen durchs Gefild,
Und wie sie scherzend sich enthaschen
Sein aufgeblühtes Bild.

Froh lächelt seine Mutter Erde
Nach ihrem langen Harm;
Sie schlingt mit jubelnder Gebärde
Das Söhnlein in den Arm.

SPRING

Now comes the Spring, that youth beguiling,
Who in all hearts must reign
And enters in and greets us smiling
On dancing feet again.

No sooner come than he is playing
Pranks often played before
On old giant Wintertime, dismaying
The poor old man once more.

He starts the little brooklets leaping
And lets the old man scold
Who held them in his icy keeping
And rigid chains of cold.

Their waves already dancing babble
And swiftly onward run,
And mock the tyrant, a gay rabble,
Now that his rule is done.

Spring laughs to see them never tarry
But noisy haste away
And playfully reflect and carry
His image flowered and gay.

His mother Earth in happy fashion
Now smiles, her long pain done,
And clasps once more with joyful passion
Close in her arms her son.

In ihren Busen greift der Lose
Und zieht ihr schmeichelnd keck
Das sanfte Veilchen und die Rose
Hervor aus dem Versteck.

Und sein geschmeidiges Gesinde
Schickt er zu Berg und Tal:
“Sagt, daß ich da bin, meine Winde,
Den Freunden allzumal!”

Er zieht das Herz an Liebesketten
Rasch über manche Kluft,
Und schleudert seine Singraketen,
Die Lerchen, in die Luft.

The naughty youth her bosom plunders,
With bold yet melting grace,
And violets and roses sunders
From their safe hiding-place;

His minions sends where'er he pleases,
To hill, dale, far or near:
"Tell all my friends, my swift-winged breezes,
That I, the Spring, am here."

He bears on chains of love's devotion
Our hearts where dread gulfs lie;
And sets his rockets in swift motion,
The skylarks, to the sky.

WALDLIEDER

I

Am Kirchhof dort bin ich gestanden,
Wo unten still das Rätsel modert,
Und auf in Grabesrosen lodert;
Es blüht die Welt in Todesbanden.

Dort lächelt auf die Gräber nieder
Mit himmlisch duldender Gebärde
Vom Kreuz das höchste Bild der Erde;
Ein Vogel drauf sang seine Lieder.

Doch kaum daß sie geklungen hatten,
Flog scheu zum Wald zurück der Wilde;
Ich sang, wie er, ein Lied dem Bilde,
Und kehrte heim in meine Schatten.

Natur! will dir ans Herz mich legen!
Verzeih, daß ich dich konnte meiden,
Daß Heilung ich gesucht für Leiden,
Die du mir gabst zum herben Segen.

In deinen Waldesfinsternissen
Hab' ich von mancher tiefen Ritze,
Durch die mir leuchten deine Blitze,
Den trüglichen Verband gerissen.

V

Wie Merlin
Möcht' ich durch die Wälder ziehn,
Was die Stürme wehen,
Was die Donner rollen

FOREST SONGS

I

I stood by yonder churchyard grounds:
Enigma moulders in the earth
And in the roses finds new birth;
Life flowers in very death's own bounds.

Upon the graves Christ turns his gaze
With heavenly meekness in his eyes,
The highest symbol men devise;
A bird sang on the cross its lays.

But hardly was the last note spent,
Into the woods the wild bird flew;
Like it, I sang Christ songs of rue,
Then to my shadows homeward went.

Nature, I flee back to your heart;
Forgive me that I turned from you
To seek to cure as ills in rue
The bitter blessings you impart.

I have, where your dark shadows sway,
From many a rift both dark and deep
Through which your lordly lightnings leap
Delusion's blindfold torn away.

V

Like to Merlin,
Through the forest I would go:
What the storm-winds blow,
What the thunder's calling,

Und die Blitze wollen,
Was die Bäume sprechen,
Wenn sie brechen,
Möcht' ich wie Merlin verstehen.

Voll Gewitterlust
Wirft im Sturme hin
Sein Gewand Merlin,
Daß die Lüfte kühlen,
Blitze ihm bespülen
Seine nackte Brust.

Wurzelfäden streckt
Eiche in den Grund,
Unten saugt versteckt
Tausendfach ihr Mund
Leben aus geheimen Quellen,
Die den Stamm gen Himmel schwellen.

Flattern läßt sein Haar Merlin
In der Sturmnacht her und hin,
Und es sprühn die feurig falben
Blitze, ihm das Haupt zu salben;
Die Natur, die offenbare,
Traulich sich mit ihm verschwisternd,
Tränkt sein Herz, wenn Blitze knisternd
Küssen seine schwarzen Haare.—

Das Gewitter ist vollbracht,
Stille ward die Nacht;
Heiter in die tiefsten Gründe
Ist der Himmel nach dem Streite;
Wer die Waldesruh' verstünde
Wie Merlin, der Eingeweihte!

And the lightning seeking,
And the trees are speaking,
As they're falling,
Would, like Merlin, know.

Joying in the tempest,
In the stormy blast
Merlin's cloak is cast
Wide to the wind's blowing;
Cleansing lightning's flowing
Round his naked breast.

Threadlike roots send deep
Oaks into the mould;
Hidden, drinking, creep
Mouths a thousandfold;
Life from secret springs emerging
Sends the tall trunks skyward surging.

Merlin lets his long locks blow
In the storm-night to and fro;
And the fiery lightnings bring
Royal oil to anoint him king;
Nature lays her secrets bare
To her brother, and with blisses
Fills his heart, as lightning kisses
With its flames his raven hair.—

Storm and lightning taking flight,
Silent is the night;
Gay, serene the sky, storm ended;
Blessed who like Merlin fated
The wood's peace has comprehended,
In its mysteries consecrated.

Frühlingsnacht! kein Lüftchen weht,
Nicht die schwanksten Halme nicken,
Jedes Blatt, von Mondesblicken
Wie bezaubert, stille steht.
Still die Götter zu beschleichen
Und die ewigen Gesetze,
In den Schatten hoher Eichen
Wacht der Zaubrer, einsam sinnend,
Zwischen ihre Zweige spinnend
Heimliche Gedankennetze.

Stimmen, die den andern schweigen,
Jenseits ihrer Hörbarkeiten,
Hört Merlin vorübergleiten,
Alles rauscht im vollen Reigen.
Denn die Königin der Elfen,
Oder eine kluge Norn
Hält, dem Sinne nachzuhelfen,
Ihm ans Ohr ein Zauberhorn.
Rieseln hört er, springend schäumen
Lebensfluten in den Bäumen;
Vögel schlummern auf den Ästen
Nach des Tages Liebesfesten,
Doch ihr Schlaf ist auch beglückt;
Lauschend hört Merlin entzückt
Unter ihrem Brustgefieder
Träumen ihre künft'gen Lieder.
Klingend strömt des Mondes Licht
Auf die Eich' und Hagerose,
Und im Kelch der feinsten Moose
Tönt das ewige Gedicht.

Night of spring! No breezes shiver;
Not the supplest grass-blade dances;
And the leaves, by the moon's glances
Deep enchanted, never quiver.
Still, the high gods' words to hearken,
Learn the laws whose end is never,
Where the oak trees' shadows darken
The seer sits, alone conceiving
And across their branches weaving
Nets of thought, secret forever.

Voices, still for other mortals,
Tuned beyond their range of hearing,
Merlin's ears are ever nearing,
Worlds of sound storm at their portals.
For the queen of elves appearing,
Or a wise and hoary Norn,
Holds, to help his mortal hearing,
To his ear a magic horn.
Pulsing life, a surging river
He hears in the tree trunks quiver;
In the branches after daytime,
Weary from their happy playtime,
Birds are sleeping, still, content.
And delighted Merlin's ear bent
Hears beneath their feathers clinging
How they dream tomorrow's singing.
Melody of moonlight pouring
Streams on oak trees and wild roses;
From where lowly moss reposes
The eternal poem is soaring.

VI

Der Nachtwind hat in den Bäumen
Sein Rauschen eingestellt,
Die Vögel sitzen und träumen
Am Aste traut gesellt.

Die ferne schmächtige Quelle,
Weil alles andre ruht,
Läßt hörbar nun Welle auf Welle
Hinflüstern ihre Flut.

Und wenn die Nähe verklungen,
Dann kommen an die Reih'
Die leisen Erinnerungen
Und weinen fern vorbei.

Daß alles vorübersterbe,
Ist alt und allbekannt;
Doch diese Wehmut, die herbe,
Hat niemand noch gebannt.

VII

Schläfrig hangen die sonnenmüden Blätter,
Alles schweigt im Walde, nur eine Biene
Summt dort an der Blüte mit mattem Eifer;
Sie auch ließ vom sommerlichen Getöne,
Eingeschlafen vielleicht im Schoß der Blume.
Hier, noch Frühlings, rauschte die muntre Quelle;
Still versiegend ist in die Luft zergangen
All ihr frisches Geplauder, helles Schimmern.
Traurig kahl die Stätte, wo einst ein Quell floß;
Horchen muß ich noch dem gewohnten Rauschen,
Ich vermisse den Bach, wie liebe Grüße,
Die sonst fernher kamen, nun ausgeblieben.

VI

The night wind's no longer streaming,
In the trees its rustle has died;
The birds on their perches dreaming,
Nestle side by side.

All is so still that the distant
Fountain's muted tone
With its water's music persistent
Fills the forest alone.

The near into silence falling,
Memories softly rise
And ghostlike, beyond recalling,
Pass us with tear-filled eyes.

That all things die and vanish
Is an old and familiar tale;
This bitter sadness to banish
Can no man's strength avail.

VII

Drowsily hang the leaves, tired of the sunlight;
All is still in the forest; only a bee still
Buzzes with drowsy zeal there by the blossom;
It too ceases its summery song and has fallen
Mayhap sound asleep in the lap of the flower.
Where in the springtime the fountain rippled and gurgled
All its happy chatter is silenced and even
Its crystal sparkle has vanished, drunk by the breezes.
Sad and bare is the spot where once a spring bubbled;
For a familiar sound of water vainly I listen,
The brooklet that sounded once from afar
Like a loved greeting, now has grown silent.

Alles still, einschläfernd, des dichten Mooses
Sanft nachgiebige Schwellung ist so ruhlich;
Möge hier mich holder Schlummer beschleichen,
Mir die Schlüssel zu meinen Schätzen stehlen,
Und die Waffen entwenden meines Zornes,
Daß die Seele, rings nach außen vergessend,
Sich in ihre Tiefen hinein erinnre.
Preisen will ich den Schlummer, bis er leise
Naht in diesem Dunkel und mir das Aug' schließt.

Schlaf, du kindlicher Gott, du Gott der Kindheit!
Du Verjünger der Welt, die, dein entbehrend,
Rasch in wenig Stunden wäre gealtert.
Wundertätiger Freund, Erlöser des Herzens!
Rings umstellt und bewacht am hellen Tage
Ist das Herz in der Brust und unzugänglich
Für die leiseren Genien des Lebens,
Denn ihm wandeln voran auf allen Wegen
Die Gedanken, bewaffnet, als Liktoren,
Schreckend und verscheuchend lieblichen Zauber.
Aber in der Stille der Nacht, des Schlummers,
Wacht die Seele heimlich und lauscht wie Hero,
Bis verborgen ihr Gott ihr naht, herüber
Schwimmend durch das wallende Meer der Träume.

Eine Flöte klang mir im Schlaf zuweilen,
Wie ein Gesang der Urwelt, Sehnsucht weckend,
Daß ich süß erschüttert erwacht' in Tränen,
Und noch lange hörte den Ruf der Heimat;
Bliebe davon ein Hauch in meinen Liedern!

Schlaf, melodischer Freund, woher die Flöte?
Ist sie ein Ast des Walds, durchhaucht vom Gotte,
Hört' ich im Traum des heiligen Pan Syringe?

All is still; my senses grow drowsy; the moss is
A pillow swelling and soft, inviting to slumber.
Here let Sleep, sweet Sleep, descend now upon me
Stealing from me the keys to my soul's treasures,
And taking its weapons out of the hands of my anger,
That my soul, forgetful of all things external,
May remember the way to the deepest depths of itself.
Praise will I give to Sleep until at last softly
It comes in this darkness and gently closes my eyelids.

Sleep, thou childlike God, thou God of childhood,
Rejuvenator without whom the world would
In a few brief hours grow old and wither;
Miraculous friend, the human heart's savior.
Ever completely surrounded and guarded by daytime
Is the heart in our bosom, entirely cut off from
Contact with life's quieter and gentler spirits.
For before it walk on all of its journeys
Our thoughts, fully and heavily armed, like lictors,
Affrighting and driving away sweet enchantments.
But in the stillness of night, in the quiet of slumber,
The soul watches alone and listens like Hero
Till in secret her god comes to join his beloved,
Swimming the billowing sea of dreams, like Leander.

Now and again there sounded a flute through my slumber,
Tones from the world primeval, awaking such yearning,
That, sweetly stirred to the depths, I wakened up tearful
And still heard for long the far call of my homeland.
Would that its tones were still alive in my verses.

Sleep, melodious friend, whence came the flute tone?
Was it some forest branch played by the godhead,
Heard I in dream the syrinx of Pan the Almighty?

IX

Rings ein Verstummen, ein Entfärben;
Wie sanft den Wald die Lüfte streicheln,
Sein welkes Laub ihm abzuschmeicheln;
Ich liebe dieses milde Sterben.

Von hinnen geht die stille Reise,
Die Zeit der Liebe ist verklungen,
Die Vögel haben ausgesungen,
Und dürre Blätter sinken leise.

Die Vögel zogen nach dem Süden,
Aus dem Verfall des Laubes tauchen
Die Nester, die nicht Schutz mehr brauchen,
Die Blätter fallen stets, die müden.

In dieses Waldes leisem Rauschen
Ist mir, als hör' ich Kunde wehen,
Daß alles Sterben und Vergehen
Nur heimlich still vergnügtes Tauschen.

IX

Now voices hush; the bright hues fade;
Caressing hands, the breezes stroke
The dying leaves from beech and oak;
I love this death so gently made.

Hence now the silent journey goes,
The day of love its course has run,
The singing of the birds is done
And dry leaves fall like amber snows.

The birds have felt the southward call;
Their hidden nests are now laid bare,
Nor need the leaves' protecting care;
Unceasingly the tired leaves fall.

Soft rustlings through the forest range
And seem, a still small voice, to say
That what we call death and decay
Is only quiet, contented change.

EITEL NICHTS!

’s ist eitel nichts, wohin mein Aug’ ich hefte!
Das Leben ist ein vielbesagtes Wandern,
Ein wüstes Jagen ist’s von dem zum andern,
Und unterwegs verlieren wir die Kräfte.
Ja, könnte man zum letzten Erdenziele
Noch als derselbe frische Bursche kommen,
Wie man den ersten Anlauf hat genommen,
So möchte man noch lachen zu dem Spiele.
Doch trägt uns eine Macht von Stund’ zu Stund’,
Wie’s Krüglein, das am Brunnenstein zersprang,
Und dessen Inhalt sickert auf den Grund,
So weit es ging, den ganzen Weg entlang.
Nun ist es leer; wer mag daraus noch trinken?
Und zu den andern Scherben muß es sinken.

ALL IS VANITY

Nothing but vanity I see at every turning.
Life is, as many men have said, a wand'ring,
Nay more, a mad, a wild pursuit, a squand'ring
Of all our powers in seeking this, that spurning.
Aye, could one reach the goal of his endeavor
At last as the same youth who one day started
His earthly course so bravely, so high-hearted,
Then one might find the game amusing ever.
But some power bears us onward hour by hour,
A pitcher at the fountain's stone edge cracking
Whose water drips in slow but steady shower
Along the track until the final drop is lacking.
No water for our lips within it guarded,
Among its fellow shards it falls discarded.

Vienna, April, 1836

I waited for my nightingale in vain today. Perhaps it is dead. It is after midnight, the time when it used to sing loudest and poured its song so deeply into my wound and awoke all my longing for you. Today it is silent; only the fountain murmurs and its waters, too, flow away without their usual song, as life does when a poet dies. There are moments when it seems in your relations with me as if the fountain of your joys which murmurs in the young life of your children would go on murmuring just as happily without me, just as here below me the fountain does without the voice of the night.

In such moments my love is not weaker, but I feel it as a burning pain which, especially in company, I hide from you behind what you call an attitude of proud scorn. And it may well happen that I shall long in such moments to escape from you and the whole world, for you have become so completely the extreme goal of my desires and emotions that I can find no other goal for my longings but in death. And this longing which I have felt very powerfully in these last days is bearable only through the wish and hope that I may find you there and that there you will no longer make me sad. Would you were with me now! Oh, if I could only once and for all convince you with my kisses that I love you beyond all measure. Then you would never again misunderstand me and sadden me.—

Reichenau, July 23, 1836

I can now measure how much my love for you has grown. It was never so hard for me to leave you as this time. If in the future I should be compelled to leave you for a really long time I should, indeed, be miserable. My life without you is a continual silent bleeding of my heart. I can work only by the most extreme exertion of my will.

Reichenau, July 27, 1836

Yes, dear Sophie, I should be able to work here, but every day I live without you is a day stolen from my life; and no mortal has ever made verses lovely enough to make up for the loss of one of your glances. When we are together again I shall watch to see whether, when you hear these mountain poems, you will not say: "These are all poems of a man seeking a sanctuary, all of them created out of a deep need, because I was not with you."

Reichenau, July 28, 1836

I shall not be able to stand it here much longer. Even though the scenery is glorious and my stay here as undisturbed and poetic as I could wish, when evening comes nothing satisfies me any longer and I only long to be with you. When I go walking in this lovely mountain region and lose myself in the view, I suddenly think of you and how it would be to be here with you; and then melancholy overwhelms me, the more painfully the lovelier the scenery and the life we might live here together. Since our separation I feel, indeed, a deep melancholy whenever I remember you such as I have never experienced before.

Vienna, August 10, 1836

Yesterday was the longest day of my life. Now I really know for the first time what fear is, torturing, restless fear. I wanted to write, but couldn't, and even today I have to force myself to write in order to keep my promise. Is she not sick? That is the only thought of which I am capable since I saw you at your window as I drove by. When you collapsed so weary and weak on the sofa and looked at me with a look of deepest suffering, my heart felt as if my whole heaven were collapsing; I was stricken to the heart and crushed. I felt a violent urge to sink at your feet, and then you told me to go and I went. If I were to lose you, could God comfort me? I cannot think of God without thinking of you, and He would open my wound even more deeply. I should die, that is certain. If He takes you away from me, He takes the very basis of my existence; He takes away food and drink from my heart; He takes away the air which I breathe; He does not want me to go on living. If only it were already 12 o'clock!

Stuttgart, September [?], *1836*

In spite of the great love with which my friends and hosts cherish me in their midst, my life here is only half a life. It fills my heart with melancholy to be incapable of returning my friends' love. My love reaches out into the distance toward you and pays no attention to all the love which closely surrounds it. I am truly sick. I am always thinking only of you and of death. I often feel seriously that my time is up. I cannot write poetry, I can take pleasure in nothing, can hope for nothing; I can only think of you and of death. Recently I wrote you to guard your health, and I myself have so little courage to live. I cannot hide from you a thought which for some time has been overshadowing my life darkly and ever more darkly. Something drives me to seek what I wish. But that will pass. When I see you again, my dearest.

Penzing, October [?], *1836*

A conversation like ours today seemed to me unusual between a man and a woman; in our case I find it good and right. It gives me great pleasure to follow your thoughts to their source, for each time I found that they flowed from the purest of springs. An understanding like this can be risked with few women; with the others one would find oneself at times in marshes and morasses where there are no flowers to be picked, but on the contrary one's foot sinks into destruction, into the sad and bottomless swamp of lost respect. Dangerous paths for others, such conversations are for us a further proof of our trust and devotion. Never hesitate to open your innermost heart to me; I have drawn each time joy and increased love from the depths of your soul. That is the way it was today.

Penzing, October [?], *1836*

My whole soul (*Gemüt*) is now as clear as the air after a thunderstorm, and I think I can see far into our future; it is a lovely future. Love is the strongest power in heaven or on earth; it created the world and preserves it and causes it to move eternally; it has taken possession of our hearts and all that is contrary to love must burn up and be annihilated like a straw cast into a burning volcano. Sophie! If there were any alien element in me which sought to break away from you, my real genuine self clung all the more firmly to you; anything else was only external thoughts, merely on the surface, and the hostile element only served to make my love stronger. It has been destroyed as everything must be which struggles against love in this world. Sophie, you have often asked me: "What are you thinking now?" And in the moments of highest bliss I had not even been thinking at all, but was submerged in my love, as I am in God when I pray. Love is beyond expression, because it is far beyond all thought. Therefore, when it is true love, no thought can injure it. Oh, Sophie, you convinced me today that nothing can harm me in your eyes, no memory. You love me, you must love me, as your greatest achievement. Because of you my dead hopes and joys have arisen again to a new and fairer life; you are my comfort, the warmth of my life, my revelation; I owe to you my reconciliation on earth and my peace in heaven. Oh, Sophie, let us hold together, faithfully, joyfully, forever, forever.

Penzing, October [?], *1836*

You wronged me when you thought that I had relapsed into my old ways, I had not and shall not. There cannot be two such terrible moods in a human heart. That is certain. There is only one devil in love, and I have renounced him. In me is a clear calm as in the air after a thunderstorm. I feel such repulsion now for certain lines of thought that I would avoid them with all my strength if they ever presented themselves again. The violence of my passion seems uncanny to me. My mistake is that I do not keep the sphere of poetry and the sphere of real life apart, but let the two become entangled. Accustomed to surrender myself to the drive of my imagination in my poetry, I do the same thing in my life, and so it comes about that in moments of self-forgetfulness this power, probably too well exercised, builds itself up and tramples destructively on its own fairest creations. I am in general a poor manager and in the economy of my psychological powers I keep too lax an accounting and too little balance and order. Here your words apply: "It's a bad business being such a poet." I am a melancholist. The compass needle of my life ever vibrates back to the pain of life. Perhaps all religion and love can do no more to help me than to transfigure the pain. But know this: that the moments of a true and holy love leave deep wounds in a human being like me. With me it is not a case of painting the surface; everything is etched in, engraved, carved. Your image and our lovely hours are etched into my heart with the sharpness and accuracy of unhappiness, for our love is unhappy.

Vienna, October 22, 1836

Your farewell rose lies beside me on the desk and is as fragrant as if today were breathing away its lovely life in the flower. Oh, it was a lovely day! I ended it when I said good-by to you in the garden. I am almost glad that I did not see you alone again afterward. After all, the undisturbed hours were over, and with them the day was over. Farewell, lovely day, you fugitive guest from a better world. I could weep for your passing. Oh, Sophie! This is a day the memory of which your heart should cling to. I shall celebrate it every year like your birthday. I have found more assurance of eternal life in communion with you than in all my study and observation of the world. When I thought in some happy hour that now the highest level of love had been reached and the moment to die had arrived because nothing lovelier could follow, each time it was an illusion, and there followed an even lovelier hour in which my love for you reached an even higher level. These ever new, ever deeper abysses of life give me assurance of its eternity. I saw in your lovely eyes today the full richness of the divine. I was happy as never before. I realized again today clearly that the soul breathes in the raising and dropping of the eyes. In such lovely eyes as yours is revealed, as in a prophetic hieroglyph, the material of which our eternal body will some day be made. When I die, I shall go from life a rich man, for I shall have beheld the loveliest of all things. Your farewell rose is as fragrant as a goodnight from you. Sleep well, dear heart. Keep the other rose as a keepsake. It was a lovely day. I love you beyond all bounds.

Penzing, October 29, 1836

If you had gotten dressed in your mourning costume half an hour earlier today, we should have had more time together. But you waited until I came. It is, perhaps, the case that you have only begun to put on mourning since I came into your life. I must admit that this symbolic coincidence depressed me.

How did you spend the evening? Mine was a complete loss. To walk home in the dreadful weather without having really talked to you made me irritable. Then, too, I kept remembering you in that black dress and I almost wished you were wearing it for me. But, no! I will carry my burden a little further, even though in doing so I pass by your grave. Not past it, but, perhaps, to your grave. I don't know. The day before yesterday was very different from yesterday. This crippled, horrible yesterday does not deserve to be called a day. One must wade through such periods to reach another happy hour. Life is a wretched business.

Vienna, February [?], 1837 (morning)

This morning I awoke out of a lovely dream with blissful thoughts of you. Love is all-powerful. Let life heap up its bothersome flotsam and jetsam on its inhospitable shore, a single wave of love, of the wide, deep and powerful sea, washes all the wreckage away, as if it had never been there. This morning I lay lonely and happy in the dark. Do you know these moments of love when the heart is in heaven and forgets every wish? Oh, you certainly know them! I had drawn you so close to me, held you so closely embraced, that every barrier was removed and forgotten.—My love is so great that my heart often gets confused and cannot grasp it and is then driven to emotions which border on insanity and wound you. Therefore, I firmly believe that there is an eternity prepared for this love where it can develop freely and completely. But even now I have moments when I can lose my self peacefully in you and in the thought that you love me. That is how it was with me this morning.

Vienna, February, [?] *1837* (*morning*)

Has all my longing and desiring attached itself to you, sweet, importunate vision? Can I find no escape from you? The whole world has become for me a frame for you, and if my seeing you were snatched from me, the frame would be empty and void. I awoke today with a violent longing for you, Sophie.

Vienna, February [?], *1837*

You are not to reproach yourself for having forced your way into my life and shaken it to its very foundations. I bless you for your coming and rejoice in the healing cataclysm. To be sure, you have cut sharply and deeply into my heart and have plowed it deeply; but you have given it a new green springtime. But any coldness from you hurts this springtime, and you ought to be more gentle to your own creation. The thought often enters my head: renounce this dependence and allow no woman such a powerful influence over your emotions; no human being on earth should dominate you thus. —But I soon repelled this thought as a traitor to my love, and gladly offered my sensitive heart again to your tender mistreatment. I beg you with all my heart not to send this thought, this rebel, back to me again; I don't want to have anything to do with it. Oh, dear heart, do not misuse your power. I beg you, dear Sophie! Your last note is so sweet and so good; it cheered me and refreshed me. Write again soon!

Vienna, March [?], *1837*

Recently you shut your lovely eyes after a lovely hour in order to keep alive in your soul the hour that had just rushed by. I should like to close my eyes forever after such an hour and go on enjoying my happiness there where a man who has known happiness is, perhaps, never again disturbed. Yesterday such an hour was granted us, an hour so full of bliss that it would be worthy of an eternal experiencing in another life. Oh, dear heart, when I left you yesterday my soul clung to you and kissed you ever and again. Dear Sophie, did you not feel it?

Vienna [*end of*] *March, 1837*

The time of our undisturbed being together hurries away. Spring approaches for nature, spring which is a winter for our love's wishes. Here, too, I see a melancholy disparity between our fate and nature. But it shall be the goal of our lives to reconcile the eternal disturbances and disharmonies by the unshakable and deep harmony of our hearts. The unhappiness of our love shall only strengthen it; perhaps, it is practice for eternity. Once we have learned to find each other in all the changes of this life, we shall, perhaps, some day at the great transformation of this life into an eternal life, find and hold each other all the more easily. Love exists not merely to propagate the species, but also, and certainly chiefly, for the sake of the eternal life of the individual. The former is denied our love; let us, therefore, hold firmly to the latter, and turn the whole force of our love into our own innermost beings and fill each other and make each other happy, and faithfully agree upon the sign which we shall give each other there in order that we may recognize each other. I will try to tone down the outbursts of my passion; I cannot control them completely. I am sailing on the highest sea, and there is no dropping an anchor there. But for the sake of your tender solicitude, I will do what I can. You are, of course, quite right that the violence of my emotions is devouring my life. It cannot be otherwise. But my prodigality gives me joy, and I would gladly die under your kisses.

Vienna, [*end of*] *April, 1837*

Last night I had a blissful dream which has re-echoed in me all day long. It cannot be described, it can only be dreamed or experienced in another life. Dear heart! Yesterday evening was, perhaps, the last lovely evening before the long, long time of disturbances which threatens our immediate future. I cannot look forward at all to spring because this time it is coming like a lovely thief. Oh, our dear winter! How gladly would I begin it all over again. We had a rich world in the midst of its harsh cold. What good do flowers and birds do me, if I can't kiss you? You have sometimes complained that your love makes you dead to all the joys of life. I make no complaint, though it affects me more than you. I am happy that you are the sole focus of my life. Perhaps he can be more easily made a beggar who has all his possessions together in one beloved heart than he for whom joy springs up everywhere, safely divided. But my happiness is the deeper and dearer to me, the more dangerous it is. Where have you been all this long while? It is already half-past seven. Do come home. It is already dark. My pen goes like a nighttime wanderer through the labyrinth of my love from which I shall never find the way out. Come! Come! Where are you staying so long? The clock goes on ticking away and reminds me how prodigally you are wasting our time. It is already quite dark, and if you do not come soon I shall be very sad.

Penzing, May [?], *1837*

You regret that you recently stepped to the window and tapped at it as I left. Don't regret it. Loving surrender is exactly what gives you your great charm and makes you irresistible. Do you think that such actions are lost on me and that I do not approve them in my heart, even though I may not show it at the moment? You have once and for all taken the risky step of loving a man of my kind, and it would be wrong in you to forsake me some day or other. A kind of melancholy pride is so characteristic of me that, if you ever let me go without a sign of love, I am capable of throwing myself into a post coach and departing without a farewell, even though my heart should break ten times at each stopping place. Oh, Sophie, remain as you were!

Penzing, May [?], *1837*

The sudden change of my moods from the highest joy to the deepest melancholy reveals to me a pathological tension in my soul. You are terribly mistaken if you think there are moments when I love you less. I love you always. But there is a darkening, a fading of my spiritual (*geistigen*) powers which I cannot describe. But you are always there. Even when I do not see you, I reach out for you in the darkness and feel you there; and if I do not feel you, then I feel through you, for you are my heart's blood. Therefore, I never have a wish that I could live without you, as you wish you could without me. Just try to live without me! You will endure it for a while and, perhaps, be happier; but suddenly you will feel homesickness for the mountain air which I have given you to breathe and from which you would then be banished into the calm, stuffy lowlands of the others. Try it!

Penzing, June 1, 1837

Your last two letters were all too brief. Can't you get back into your old sweet habit of chattering away, my dear, my dearest heart? Did I frighten you recently with my crossness? No hand has ever taken such a harsh hold of your life as mine. There is no changing this. I love you so limitlessly that you carry me to the extreme limits in happiness as in depression. You hold the whole lyre of my heart in your power; you can make it vibrate from the gentlest whispering to the most violent storm with a pressure of your finger. I pay homage to you as I could not do to any other human being; but I do overstep the bounds of politeness with you which I would not flout with any one else. My love knows no law but the law it gives itself. You must judge me from this standpoint, and you do, too. Today you were so charming you swept me into an emotional tumult. It was a blissful evening—more so than any preceding one. Good-night, my dear.

Penzing, June 11, 1837

—Your sadness at my leaving shakes me deeply. Oh, dear, deep, holy heart! Why should you be surprised that I prefer you to Marie? I can visualize her in all her worth and add in my imagination perfection to all her charming traits, and yet I look at her, compared to you, with a quite calm pleasure, for you outshine her a thousand and a thousand times in your humble majesty. You say that your being harassed with domestic cares will lower you in my esteem. If you knew how dear each and every household utensil which your hand touches is to me, how in your hands things become ennobled, intimate and dear to me, things which formerly only bothered me, you would not speak slightingly of your domestic activities. Your way of life just as it is suits me. Sophie, I reverence you as I reverence no other human being, and I love you as one can only love you. Console yourself at the thought of our separation; think of next winter, think of the remainder of the summer which we are, after all, going to spend together. Trust my love! I shall come as soon as I can; longing for you will give wings to my work and make it child's play. Do not worry lest the strain be too much for me. Doesn't the tiredest horse trot quicker when it's homeward bound? And should I not hurry to you over stock and stone along the road of my literary activity, sweet homeland of my soul?

Penzing, June [?], *1837*

Why shouldn't your last letter have given me pleasure? After all it was one of your dearest, your loveliest. You must not hesitate to express a wish which is only a gentle echo of my loud longing. Today will always remain dear to me. Both heavens were sweet, the one in the air above and the one in your heart. I said at dinner that I should like to store up today's air for the whole year, and I thought as I said it that I should like to preserve this soft, sweet breathing of your soul for the whole of my life. Your charm is in full bloom. When I look at you, my soul begins to ring like bells. You are created out of the material of which the best core of creation is made. Your being is creative magic. If only I could tell what I am trying to say! I mean you are at one and the same time the sweetest dream and the firmest reality. Oh, Sophie, Sophie! You looked at me several times today in such a way that I could not but think of your death. Your soul was so fully revealed in your open eyes, as if it wanted to flee away from me. You have magic moments. I rejoice that I am the only one who sees them. They are the loveliest thing in my life. Good night, my Sophie.

Penzing, June 14, 1837

Keep firmly in your memory today's walk at twilight, when impatience comes over you and sadness overpowers you. Our love is in part an unhappy one, and we will play to our life's end, unshaken and courageous, the silent secret tragedy in which no one acts and no one watches but our bleeding hearts. Perhaps, yes, certainly, we shall some day be rewarded by the applause of the heavenly audience. I have moments when I could die of the pain of our lot; but I also have others in which our unhappiness is precious to me, when I think that you would, perhaps, love me less if your love had not grown to maturity in the midst of dangers and pain. Do hearts, perhaps, have to be cut open, if they are to grow together? We have joined the bleeding edges and must hold them firmly together lest we bleed to death. Oh, I intend to hold you! And you will hold me, I know.

Linz, June 18, 1837

The coach stops here briefly and I am going to write down for you some of the thousand thoughts and feelings which have been affecting me since yesterday evening. That you waited for me with your children and waved good-by so tenderly until I lost sight of you, made an impression on me which will never leave me. You hurried after the coach a while, but it hastened away with me faster than you; I felt as if your dear form was left ever farther behind, as if I were running away from my happiness which tried in vain to follow me. The farther behind I left you, the tighter did I feel the chain binding me to you. Never was a journey so irksome to me as this one. I travel through lovely country without taking the slightest interest in it. Oh, dear, flat, dusty Penzing—you are dearer to me than all the Alps of this world. My love for

Sophie has alienated me even from nature whenever I have to enjoy it alone. If I were with you in a forest with no one to disturb us, I should understand and love nature as never before. I am very, very lonely. I face the coming days in the dullest of bad moods. The world lies soulless before my eyes. Oh, Sophie, my whole being inclines toward you and can never be moved to a different position. Every drop of my blood moves only in thoughts of you, in painful longing for you. The separation from you, the leave-taking with all its fears, upset me physically. My whole physique has revolted against this separation. Violent headaches and nausea accompanied me as far as Sighardskirchen. There I got out and, indeed, thought I could not go on. I felt a violent revulsion, horrible, incomprehensible. Then I got better. A man being sent into exile may well feel as I do. Even the knowledge that my journey is taking me to friendly arms does not help. I have no taste for any pleasure without you. I have fallen completely under your spell, and it is good that I have.——

Salzburg, June 19, 1837

I am sitting in front of the Ship Inn in Salzburg on a bench writing you. I arrived an hour ago. We left Linz yesterday at 7 P.M. A violent thunderstorm broke about 11, one of the wildest. Uninterrupted flashes and crashing peals of thunder and with it all sheets of rain. We stopped in Wels till it was over. As I looked out into the flashes of lightning I kept feeling I was going to see you and your children. That vision never leaves me, it has a melancholy magic. My traveling companion, Count Pajacsevich, thought you very lovely and would not believe the children were yours. In my lonely hours I shall conjure up the vision very often and find joy and sadness in it.

It is rainy weather. The mountains are as wrapped in melancholy as my heart. But it will grow cheerful again much later than they. My Stuttgart friends aren't going to have very much in me!

Stuttgart, June 27, 1837

I cannot allow myself to visualize the distance that lies between us, so frightened do I become. The absolute impossibility of seeing you in an hour has something horrible about it. How long an hour can turn out to be! And it's a matter of five days! Stuttgart is sickeningly far from Vienna! Very beautiful roses are blooming in the garden. I could not possibly bring you a blooming rose. Two lovers should never be so far apart that they cannot bring each other a rose still fresh and blooming. But you'll receive a little rose from me in all its freshness when I come, my true love. Fate can never again separate us so far that I could not bring you this rose preserved in its fullest freshness. Sweetheart, good night.

Stuttgart, July 2, 1837

—No time ever went so slowly as this for me. My friends overwhelm me with love; I return it from the bottom of my heart, but my longing for you can be satisfied and quieted by nothing in this world. This is all very fine, my heart says, but I lack Sophie, my dear, fair, irreplaceable Sophie. I have learned something about myself. I am, I note, much less polite and considerate to those around me than I used to be. Is it because everything else seems unimportant to me compared with my longing and unfulfilled love?

Stuttgart, July 3, 1837

—I am not able to write you a real letter; my own words and thoughts irritate me. I suffer from a remarkable dearth of the latter. I am too far from the dear spring from which I am accustomed to draw my thoughts and feeling. I envy the workers in your garden who can see and greet you every day!

Stuttgart, July 7, 1837

Dear Emilie [Reinbeck] suspects the sorrow and longing of my heart. I sat beside her on the sofa this evening wrapped up in you and completely lost in my thoughts of you. She noticed it and showed a silent but deep sympathy. Sophie, Sophie, you are the loveliest greeting God has sent me. I should listen eternally only to you and draw you into myself with all my power. If only I had a handful of the dust you walked on as you followed my coach in Penzing. How long it is since I have looked into your eyes! This loss can never be made good. If I sacrifice my heart's blood to my poetic activity and give up a fragment of my life with each poem in an honest expending of my best efforts, all this is after all nothing compared to the sacrifice I make in doing without you. My whole soul aches for you. Oh, my dear! And if my works are no good, it drives me to despair that I have sacrificed so much for them. Dear Sophie! This flat paper and this weak pen! If I could only engrave deeply in something firm and lasting: dear Sophie, my heart, my love.

Stuttgart, July 10, 1837

Lotte Hartmann played some melodies of Bellini on the piano this evening. I should avoid music when I am away from you, for it awakes in me a longing and a sorrow of devouring intensity. I feel how my heart contracts painfully and goes on beating only reluctantly. A heavy weight lies on me again.

Stuttgart, July 17, 1837

My life here is the same day after day. But I think that the monotony makes the separation more bearable than it would be if my life were full of change and activity. At least I have undisturbed leisure to think of you and am not forced to keep myself keyed up to a social activity which has never been so irksome to me as at present.—I am busy with the revision of my poems. I find plenty of places that need polishing. If only *Savonarola* were finished for your birthday! It is already looking forward to finding itself in your dear hands, for it owes to you most of the good passages there are in it. My writing goes badly. If a thought does stir here and there in my mind, it soon withers before it has ripened. I shall bring with me a dry bouquet of flowers, my thoughts, all too early withered, and shall let your presence bring them back to life again, as in one of those warm springs which cause flowers dipped into them to bloom again.

Stuttgart, July 20, 1837

We had a lovely musical evening tonight. My favorite Schubert fantasia which I so often heard in Penzing was played, then some of my songs, quite successfully set to music, were sung. I was deeply moved and still am. Every note seemed to be an accusation that I had left you. I have already been away from you over four weeks, the twelfth part of a year, and who knows what fraction of our lives. We shall die at the same moment, shall we not, my love? I cannot believe that after your death a drop of my blood would be so disloyal as to continue its activity; every one would renounce its allegiance to life and go to sleep. And if I were to die, you would also not live much longer. Our love is not merely feeling, will, need; what unites us is more than all these things. I cannot give it a name. Our souls overlap completely; one of them would grow cold without the other and bleed to death. Sophie, take this kiss!

Stuttgart, July 27, 1837

All day long it has been extremely warm; this evening we had music in all the heat. None of the things I heard were able to stir me as they used to do.

My mood is very queer. It will be better for you not to write me at all if you are going to write as you did last time. The letter breaks off so abruptly at the end that I still feel its effect in every nerve. I read it again today; it lies on my desk like a block of ice that won't melt.

Stuttgart, August 6, 1837

I have been working all day; I wrote Max [von Löwenthal] and you and at 8 o'clock went walking in the Palace Park. The sky was gloomy and sultry, the shadowed paths dark and lonely, and my heart was sad. As I walked, my whole past life rolled in front of my feet like a tangled ball of yarn which I kept kicking ahead of me until it got entangled in some bush or other. Where are my dearest hours, those spent with you? Will they ever come again? My poems, what are they? Bloody tatters from a wretched bandage. Sleep well. I feel wretched.

Stuttgart, August 9, 1837

Today I took an hour's walk out of Stuttgart. There lies in a lonely valley with meadows and woods a very remote pond with sedge and frogs. A good place for me and my thoughts to visit. The pain I feel because of you is absolute; it cannot be assuaged; it's beyond that. You are not my wife; this is the very deep, honorable wound which will go on bleeding as long as a drop of blood flows in me. A sorrow which cannot be assuaged exactly suits your nature and mine; we could not escape it. I see the lines of suffering around your lips. Let us suffer, let us love, eternally.

Stuttgart, August 11, 1837

A very violent thunderstorm plays an accompaniment to my writing. Uninterrupted sheets of flame, as if a flash of lightning were standing still, makes the night bright. An expert portrait-painter should be able to paint a portrait by these flashes. I at least have painted your portrait thus on my heart by the flaming lightning of my passion. And I have caught the likeness well, a dear, lovely portrait. That was a terrible crash of thunder, a smashing, angry cracking, as if the devil were having a tooth pulled. A strong jaw, a strong hand! To see your face once again by these flashes and then never more. Oh, God, give me Sophie!

Stuttgart, August 13, 1837

This was the day of my birth. Thirty-five years ago this was a day of terror and joy for my mother, like no other day in her life, for my birth was extremely painful and dangerous, and I was from the first moment of my life the thing she loved most. She has long been in her grave. She left me behind as her preordained legacy to you. You may not enter into your heritage. And yet I have had a tremendous impact upon your life, perhaps transformed it into sorrow. My mother is guiltless in this. But she will rejoice in our unhappiness, in our love. But after all I am content to bleed secretly for you.

Stuttgart, August 14, 1837

I am in the worst possible of moods. That sort of irritable disgust, that giving up of all hope for and joy in the future.

Stuttgart, August 19, 1837

I have read your letter over and over again today and found in it only an upset mood and a painful tension. Can I give you any proof of my love but my word? If that does not satisfy you, I have nothing else and you deserve nothing else. At least I am beyond lying, even though my faults are many and great. It is really better to give up corresponding entirely than to spoil even the happiness we find in our longing.

Stuttgart, August 23, 1837

Like a November day on the Hungarian steppes is the mood that lies on my heart. Everything I undertake and do is inexpressibly desert and empty and stale. My earthly life has a hole in it through which the best part falls. I lack you, that is the unhappiness which is so sun-bright that my eyes hurt and my tears start when I look at it. What am I doing here any way? Playing empty tunes for the hordes of irreligous good-for-nothings? If I were a blacksmith and you my wife, I should at least know that I had not lived in vain. It's all a ghastly mess.

Stuttgart, August 25, 1837

The separation from you is a creeping poison. A deep disgust with life has taken possession of my whole being and gnaws at my life from all sides and makes it a misery. Today I have been thinking a lot about death, not with bitter defiance and stubborn longing, but as desirous of grasping the hand of a good friend. This is the result of my empty life. My poetry too seems more and more pitiful to me, the more I think about it. May God forgive me for working for his cause less zealously when I am without you. I am just sick, I am unhappy without you, and shall be happy again only with you or never.

Stuttgart, August 27, 1837

Again a very sad day without a single happy heartbeat. I am almost afraid that this depression will take such hold on me that I shall suffer from it for a long time. It is a case of vexation eating into my life, of a corrosion of all my joys. I am a very unhappy man. What will the future bring me? Does it still hold anything in store for my life? To see you again will be lovely but painful, for in the first minute of our being together we shall beat ourselves against the iron barriers until blood flows—nothing—

Stuttgart, September 3, 1837

Lately I have written you no cheerful, and hardly a loving, word. You know me well enough to excuse me. The depression caused by our separation has taken from me the last thing which can make it more bearable, the ability to create for you, so far from me, a tangible sign that I do after all live with you because I love you above everything. Depression is the worst condition of the soul for it dulls the soul and turns it into a morass. You can't imagine how stupid I have become. I cannot talk about anything, because nothing gives me pleasure and almost nothing irritates me any longer except the fact that I am not with you. Although I had foreseen a sad period of separation, I did not, before I left Penzing, have any presentiment of how intense the vexation and melancholy would really be. Besides I feel I am ungrateful to my friends here, who take the greatest delight in my being here. God knows, I love them with all my heart, but this love cannot achieve a creative expression in me at this time.

Augsburg, September 12, 1837

The coach stops here for four hours; I am somewhat tired from the journey in this heat and yet every hour of delay burns like fire in my soul. How I have been thinking of you all day. Joyfully and yet so anxiously. I am almost afraid to reach the place to which all my longing draws me. Are you well? I torture myself. How will you receive me? Will you be cross because I did not write? Oh, dear heart, do not be! These alien, calculated letters which have passed between us have not brought about a good result. That is not our language. It is better to remain wordless and quiet than to raise one's voice and yet say nothing.

Vienna, September 20, 1837

—The fact that I am so vain in my relations with you as to want to show you everything that I think and speak and write is, if one looks at it correctly, really not vanity but merely an expression of the great desire which directs my whole life: to give myself to you completely.

Penzing, September 22, 1837

Today you were again quite cheerful, dear Sophie, and have done my heart good. I rejoice when we forget our fate and are as happy as children playing in a desert or on graves—here with the withered flowers, there with the empty cup—until all of a sudden they realize their forsaken state and cry for a drink of water. Let us often be like such children and gladly lose ourselves in happy forgetfulness and, if we wake up, let us bear the forsaken state and our thirst patiently. Dear, dear Sophie, dear, noble, sweet woman, sleep well!

Penzing, September 24, 1837
(*the evening before her birthday*)

I await with deep emotion this day which has become more important in my life than any other. My deepest lament and my immeasurable happiness are bound up with this lovely day. It is my second Christmas. Your birth will have an effect beyond my earthly life upon my eternity. I am completely sure of this. Thank God for this day! May we often spend it together in the future. I have grown better through your influence. You overrate me, but your high opinion of me is good for me, for it forces me to work seriously at making myself better in order not to fall short of the image you have of me. The greatest reward for all that which I may still achieve will be the flowers that spring up in your lovely soul; in your soul, too, I find the sharpest punishment for every wasted moment of my life. You have become for me an angel of saving grace, but also an angel of punishment. I am yours with all my hopes, desires and works. Wherever I feel God's strong hand I am also aware of your dear hand, and often cannot tell the difference between them. Oh, Sophie, you are the heart of my life, which comes from you and flows back to you. I am yours eternally.

Penzing, October 8, 1837

You ended this day, which was a lovely one, with an unkindness. As we were going in to supper, you broke off our conversation coldly and almost defiantly. What was it? I don't know, but I do know that I was going to write you many things today which I cannot express now. The happier I am, the more sensitive I am. The ending of the day upsets me. You said you thought my face was false, as I sat beside you; like a cat, you said. I hope you have said that sort of thing for the last time, for that is a point where I tolerate no joking, dear Sophie. No human being stands high enough for me to find it worth while to be false to him; and on the other hand you stand too high in my esteem for me ever to be false to you. You would have heard much sweeter and softer words in place of these harsh and sharp words, if you had but granted me a kindly look.

I feel it a painful thing to have to defend my character to you, even jokingly. Do not humiliate me even teasingly. This is an injury which always draws blood, even when it but scratches the surface, a wound which even you could not heal if it ever cut deeper.

You have often accused me of being proud, and I cannot deny the accusation. Even my love, completely as it has filled my heart, could not rid me of my pride but united with it in a sisterly fashion. I love you because I can be proud of you, for I feel how noble you are. But you were in a rather haughty mood today.—

October 20, 1837

You are a fool and I am a fool. To take a wild run in order to leap over it and then to turn back at the edge of the deep, dark pit, and again to take a run and again to turn back! If that is not one of the tortures of hell! But hell is not so sophisticated. Sophie, at this moment I could do something very sad. A moment ago I was gay. We gamble with life, we cheat it, and it will nail our hands to the table. I would gladly die right now. I feel strongly that I am ripe for death. There is tumult within me. My life seems extremely suspect to me. It is roasting me at a slow fire. My life is tricky, it is a traitor. Why did we ever get to know each other? To test each other in our love? To bring sadness to each other? Shall we find what we seek only on the other side?

Penzing, October 21, 1837

Your words tonight flowed like balm into my heart. Our mutual suffering shall be holy to us. Yes, dear, noble, sweet Sophie, I do not rail at these hours nor regret that I found you. Such hours storm upon my heart with such a superabundance of joy and sorrow that the poor confused thing does not know whether to bleed or laugh, and could easily despair in its heaven; but they are the best in my life.—If I had not found you, I should never have learned what it means to be loved by a woman whose worth is so great that my unhappiness is my dearest possession. I have never dreamed of a joy for which I would exchange this unhappiness. A glimpse into your soul is not too dearly bought with the most painful renunciation, even though it means a struggle to the day of my death.

Penzing, October 29, 1837

I have been sad all day and now, as I go to bed, my sadness is at its height. If I could only ensure that I had merely passed through your life like a light breeze, I should, perhaps, wish this were my last night. But you would mourn, perhaps, for a long while, for I have cut deeply into your life. Your worst as well as your best hours came from me, and mine from you. Happiness and unhappiness have bound us closely together; we must endure to the end. This bond must never be torn apart. Earth shall have nothing firmer than our love. In this firmness our love affirms its justification and its sanctity. I am completely yours. Disturbances from outside and now and again a vexation from inside shall never make my love falter. My heart may suffer from these things but not my love, which is deeper than my heart. Its roots go through my heart into God who will preserve us. Often I am close to despair, but it will not get a real hold on me because you are so good and noble. This lifts me above my despair again and again and gives me joy. Good night, dear Sophie.

[*1837*]

Beloved, I have not ceased thinking of you for a moment today. My heart is an eternal melancholy longing for you. If I could not ever again come to see you, I would go to your house and kiss the stones at night. Yesterday you again affected me with the full power of your being. It was so hard to leave you; I have dreamed of you so sweetly; I look forward so impatiently to our dear seven o'clock.—The longer I know you, the more charming, deeper and inexhaustible I find you; you are to me a lovely mystery to which I must devote myself eternally. Oh, Sophie, I never find my contact with you a stale routine; each day I find myself stirred by you in an ever new and unexpected fashion; and in your love I have come to understand that a human being can, perhaps, become accustomed to hell, but certainly never to heaven.

Penzing, November 21, 1837

Do not forget this hour. It makes up a thousandfold for all we have suffered. Even though I was not permitted to possess you completely, I had after all more than my loveliest dreams ever believed possible. How rich you are; how much you can give, if you still hold back so much. And if you should give me all, it would not be all; I should still find ever new and deeper depths in your magic being.

Penzing, November 28, 1837

Everything in me is darkened. Fear is the worst state of mind.—It would a horrible cruelty on your part not to do the utmost toward getting well again. You have bound my whole life and activity to you. I say it in deadly earnest. The mere thought of your death poisons the world for me. I have brought my passion for you to maturity, I let it grow to full stature without hindrance; it would have been sinful of me if I had not thrown my whole life into this love, for it is my deliverance and my salvation. Now, however, it stands face to face with me so powerfully that I am frightened. I have grown accustomed to receiving the best and holiest in me from your hands. My piety is, perhaps, a child who cannot live without this mother. Take good care of yourself. So much depends on you.

Penzing, December 8, 1837

The wish to have my own hearth and my own family, you say, might suddenly awaken in me and make me susceptible to someone's charms, etc. As for the hearth, I do not want it if you are not my loving housewife, and, as for children, I want none unless you have borne them. How often must I repeat that all such wishes have meaning for my heart only through you? An hour like yesterday evening is more to me than home, hearth and children with another woman or, as you put it, the other woman. I have reread your note. You write: "Your life is forfeit to me." The words stirred me joyfully. It is as if heaven had said that my life was forfeit to it. Keep firm hold on your prey as the world calls what is yours by rights. I shall not clasp you in a slack grasp, you can count on that. The eagle has you in its talons—you must go with him, for if he lets you go you will fall wounded or dead. Such a flight is not to be treated lightly.

Penzing, January 7, 1838

You should not have demanded that I write today. All my lost desires and hopes pile up around me until I should like to bury my head in the earth to hide from them. Oh, Sophie! What good are these verses I make in my lonely study? Unsatisfying activity! If you were my wife, I should do everything better, and what I have done would please me better. As it is, both fill me with misery whenever I visualize fully the happy life I have lost, and then feel myself driven by my fate to seek a substitute for it in my writing. I would trample my works underfoot, if ever they imagined they were comforting me for your not being mine.

Penzing, January 28, 1838

—You shall not regret being as tender and all mine as you were in these last few days. I am rich and can reward you. Look around you in the wide circle of your acquaintances to see whether you can find one who can match me in emotional power. My heart has been aflame for you for three years now and you cannot show me the tiniest particle of ash which has fallen from the fire, because here no earthly fuel is being consumed, but only that which my soul gives to be burned. Sophie! Remember what you possess and remain eternally strong and fresh in your love.

Penzing, January 28, 1838 (*evening*)

When some day I am dead and you read these notes of mine your heart will feel pain. These notes are the most precious things I have written. As I wrote them, the words sprang from my heart to the paper without reflection, as a bird flies from its nest. Anyone who would understand me must read these notes. But no one except you may know me. Do you know me? You do not and even though I shall write many more of them, you will not know me until I am dead. Why not? You said recently that I was different every day. Whether the wind blows from the east or from the west, no matter how it may change, is it not always the same air? Yet no one knows me as you do. I do not know you either. I only have a partial knowledge of what you are. But what little inkling I do have is dearer to me than all that which I know in this world. I take a draught from your deep, sweet being, and that is enough to intoxicate me. When I kiss you, that is best of all.

Penzing, February 8, 1838

I should like to be able to keep this joyfulness alive in you. Let us not talk about it much, for it has always been shy and fugitive. There are days when the heart is more transparent than usual. Our last days were of that kind, and you saw in me and I in you more clearly what is happening in us. There is a quiet, secret activity and creation going on in my heart as if my soul were carefully and lovingly preparing itself for its whole future. This process goes on day and night, working and dreaming. And it is the same with you, and some day we shall, perhaps, be startled to see fully the treasure that our faithful souls have been amassing. I can't think it is otherwise when—for example, today—I look deeply and see how for quite a time now everything has grown surer, firmer, better guarded, more spiritual, more lovely. This is the secret activity of our immortal part. No diminution! No lost springtime! No sudden autumn! Here Saturday must come after Sunday. Oh, Sophie! If we grow old together, we shall grow ever younger. In your kisses is the freshness of eternal morning. Sweetheart!

Penzing, March 5, 1838

Yes, it is a good fortune for a poet to have a beloved like you. You are the one with whom I want to be, my love, my fame, my church, all in one lovely form. Every day I feel a breath of greater reconciliation and calm breathe into my heart from you, and my whole being grows stronger in you. That is why I shuddered when you smiled at me threateningly this evening. To be cast out from my possession of you would be for me the height of eternal sorrow. Oh, it cannot be! If at times you question whether I am worthy of love, think less of that than of the fact that my life is attached to you with all its fibers and lives only through you; then you will be made proof against any temptation to abandon me. If I were alone with you on a desert island, I should work just as zealously because you would be listening to me. You could compensate me for all the other things I value, as long as you love me.

Penzing, May 4, 1838 (?)

My anxious awaiting of the separation so soon to come has made my whole being weak. These six quick months with all the lovely evenings vanish before our eyes. All over and gone! Interwoven with them were some bad hours, but in my memory even they show to your advantage and as a reproach to me. Out of all the interruptions, misunderstandings and hurt feelings your love has come unweakened and victorious, and it appears to me all the more firmly established. I shall attempt as well as I can in my loneliness to master all the gnawing self-accusations that have been left in my heart. One thought will certainly help me to conquer them: the honest conviction that, whenever I hurt you, it was always a case of my passion playing tricks on me. I never for an instant grew cold toward you and, therefore, I was sometimes swept into a violence that upset you when you seemed to be cold to me. I often think after I have calmed down: This sweet young woman has her proud high spirits and these, arising from the consciousness of her love and power, should give me pleasure rather than upset me because she is, in such moments, giving expression to her childlike trust in my heart. But I take everything coming from you so to heart, so seriously, so literally, that your quite innocent teasing seems important in my eyes and threatening. I cannot take a joke in matters of love. Come, tell me, am I too old for you? I can no longer be playful with you; everything turns at once to deadly earnest. I know only too well this attitude is stiff, awkward, old.

I grew sad as the trunks for your journey were being carried out of the house. They stand piled outside the door like the coffins of our lovely days. Oh, dear Sophie!

Penzing, May 7, 1838

—How deeply everything connected with you has stamped itself on me. I feel as if I have been living close to you an eternity and then again I look back to last winter as a brief, blissful hour. You are, perhaps, for the first time feeling painfully all the places at which you have grown to be a part of me, are for the first time becoming keenly aware of the threads of the bond that binds us together, now that fate is beginning to tear at them. Our love and our unhappiness will draw nourishment and strength from what has happened and what may happen. If I tell you we shall remain faithful to each other, I am expressing it inadequately. Faithfulness is a voluntary loyalty to another person; that without which the heart cannot go on living is more than a matter of faithfulness. You understand me, Sophie, because you think the same way. Oh, how your eyes shone when you saw me coming today. I had no eyes for the lovely spring, you fairest of all!

Penzing, May 10, 1838

—You were right to be dissatisfied with my mood of yesterday and today. Once again I had an attack of that stubborn, brooding defiance which sometimes makes me stand too stiffly and harshly on my two feet vis-à-vis my destiny. My unhappiness is already determined and the very logical outcome of the circumstances. I realized this long ago and most keenly in our relationship. For four years now my unhappiness has confronted me, immovable, and continually keeps reminding me of the joys I might have had with you and have lost forever. The sum total of what I have lost grows larger with every passing hour and my fate worse. If my moral strength does not grow in proportion my downfall is assured.

If I could ever be caught up so vividly and passionately in a poetic project that I seemed to think of you less, you should rejoice in such seeming unfaithfulness. For me this would be a cure at the eternal healing spring which would pour new strength into my heart to bear my lot firmly. From it I should return home to your dear heart all the more joyful and stronger in my love.—As yet there is little hope of my taking such a cure. My painful longing for you is exercising its full rights and at this moment our still, deserted house surrounds me in all its sadness. Good night, my little Sophie. I kiss you a thousand times.

Stuttgart, June 22, 1838

—I have often felt an urge to write you but have not done so. This has come about in a queer fashion. For the first time since our love began, I have felt it necessary to spare myself. I had often taken up my pen to write you but felt a queer hesitancy to plumb the depths of my heart lest I call forth a powerful depression which might carry me too far. I owe it, indeed, to our love to spare my heart and with it my life a little. But it is less this than a fear of the demon who sometimes knocks at my door. I am seemingly cheerful.——When we have reached a certain high point of melancholy, we do not follow up one single painful emotion but let it go, because we do not wish to lose our vision of the painful totality but want to preserve a certain sad composure which can coexist quite well with our seeming external cheerfulness.

Stuttgart [*no date*]

Your last letter had a soothing effect on me for it showed that you were calm. I cannot wish you to be anything but calm, for only through calmness can you preserve yourself for me; I must lose you in a certain sense in order not to lose you.

Stuttgart [*no date*]

I sometimes—and very much so today—seem to myself like a bird of passage which has gone astray and been left behind, which has missed the southward flight of its brothers and so is now fluttering alone in an autumnal and alien world. I should not write you at all, for what I write cannot possibly give you any pleasure.

Any one who has a feeling for history cannot but, even if personally he had not been pushed down by a harsh fate into the sunken roads of melancholy, cannot but, I say, feel a deep sadness. Waste, omission, irretrievable omissions, and the failure of the fairest plans—these are what a lover of history finds everywhere in history and in nature. One should not be too hard on the so-called conservatives without having carefully studied their case beforehand. It is striking that the most thoughtful men of our age—like Leo, Görres, Baader, Schelling, and others—stretch their arms toward the past, that their desires are somewhat backward-looking. Such geniuses have, in my opinion, a deep-seated awareness of the failure of the divine purposes in history which drives them to swim against the current. They sense that the creating, shaping, weaving hand of nature (and history, which is the same thing) suddenly trembled as it was working on the finest and fairest fabric of the past, that the thread fell out of its hand and the happiness of nations and ages was thus irretrievably lost. So they are driven by a powerful instinct to go back and seek the fallen thread and join it again to the fabric. This is, perhaps, the most moving and tragic fault and mistake of great natures.

The history of mankind is repeated in concentrated form in the history of the individual human being. I am aware of what I have omitted to do, wasted, done wrongly, and that is the source of my trouble.

You appeared to me as the lovely, full, unfathomably painful embodiment of my ruined happiness. Omitted! Lost! Oh, Sophie, I must break off. My unhappiness makes me dizzy when I think what you are.

Stuttgart [*no date*]

—My letters to you, i.e., what I am scribbling in this notebook, won't please you particularly. Not as if you had no taste for my way of philosophizing; but you don't like my starting with the universal history of humanity and arriving by a circuitous route around the whole world at the quiet nook of our love. At present this way just suits me; it does me good and is comforting when I recognize in my private unhappiness the family trait which moves through the generations of poor humanity. My unhappiness is my dearest possession since it comes from you, and I like to observe it in the transfiguring light of a universal destiny.

Stuttgart [*no date*]

I look forward indescribably to our seeing each other again. You will probably find me different from what you may be expecting. I have lived a long time without you and in this period my life has turned its force into the roots rather than into the flowers and leaves, which just won't grow when you are not with me. Thus my appearance has naturally suffered and I shall appear before your eyes stamped with all the marks of one who has suffered from loneliness.

A sudden change in my circumstances, especially in my external state, was always painful to me; I like to let my heart ring out like bells. This was often the cause of my hurting your feelings—. I had to watch myself in the first few days and weeks here lest I say Sophie instead of Emilie or Julia; especially, when I wanted to say 'dear Emilie.' Certainly, I genuinely love the latter, but my blood continued to pulse in your direction, just as the waves of a lake after a strong wind still surge in the wind's direction even when it is no longer blowing.

Whenever I come to Stuttgart I find that my feelings for the few friends who were once a source of delight to me are dead. I then have to get a firm grip on myself lest all my attentiveness and good manners go by the board.

Vienna, August 24, 1838

You have no idea how I love you, and it becomes clear to me only when I think that I might lose you. Then I see myself wandering astray in the future, a man lost beyond rescue and breaking down completely. It is terrible to be so dependent on the cold, inexorable whims of nature. Nature has made you so fair and sweet and brought us together; who knows how long it will leave you on earth. I tremble when I see you in its hand and am not able to snatch you away from it if it wills to take you away. Oh, if I only had the certainty that I could cling tightly to you and remain with you in death. Sophie, dear Sophie, even in death we will fight with all our powers against being separated, shall we not? After all, we already have our heaven if we have each other.—When I see you I am much calmer about your health, but here, away from you, fear haunts me continuously. If I could only get away from here, or you would come soon.

Vienna, September 30, 1838

—As I left today you said I should, perhaps, hesitate to marry you and so lose my freedom. My freedom! It has already been pretty well curtailed. I have neglected my will in this period of our love. I have such an idolatrous fear of any such emotion that I stifle in the bud any stirring of my will, as if it were criminal. I have never seriously called a halt to the storm of my passion. If I ever should, I should certainly be calmer and safe. Sometimes I have felt that there was a power sleeping in me which I only needed to call up in order to stand with one leap on the old ground of freedom, but I feel a sense of horror at the very idea.

Such reckless courage seems satanic to me, and yet it exists within me, I must admit. You feel this, too, though darkly, and that is, perhaps, part of the power which binds you to me. If you search carefully in your own heart you will find that you believe firmly that I am irrevocably chained to you, but that you none the less hold me as your *voluntary prisoner,* while I am convinced that you have hidden in your heart no power of will sufficient to break your chains. If we should come to a parting of our ways, you *might* want to leave me, but you *cannot*. I *might* want to leave you, but I do not want to, just because you cannot. That is the powerful powerlessness of the woman and the powerless power of the man. Here lies, even though at first glance you may find it a mere splitting of hairs, a true, deep-going difference between our sexes, and on it one could build up a whole theory of love.

I delight in letting myself be tossed on the violent surges of passion and in throwing my oars into the flooding waters and rather using my arms to hold you tightly to my heart.—

Even though I know that you cannot will to do anything against our love, I sometimes fear that the bonds which hold you may loosen of themselves, and you should be very careful to avoid giving me the slightest pretext for such a fear.

Vienna, October 16, 1838

A violent change in the weather upsets a sensitive body, and a sensitive soul is injured by a sudden and violent change in external conditions. When the soul has just been dissolved in ecstasy and is suddenly contracted and painfully shaken by an icy spasm, there is the danger that the spasm will develop into a deadly rigidity from which it cannot again awake to joy. There has been left in my soul by the last few days something like a paralysis in a state of dead depression. I am, therefore, not in a state to explain to you what hurt me so deeply and why. I am too weary either to reproach you or to plead with you.

Vienna, October [*?*], *1838*

My old emotional extravagance still holds me firmly in its grip. I recently said to you: "Free me!" But I did not mean it seriously. Whenever I tell myself to break free, it is also mere empty words. Even though it is unwise of me to make my existence completely dependent on you, I gladly admit that without you my world would fall to pieces.

Kierling, October 27, 1838

I have reread the notes I wrote yesterday and find that they are quite correct. If it is no longer as it once was it has ceased to exist. If love no longer fills your whole being, it has departed forever; for that is exactly what love is: that it fills not only the human being's breast but the whole world, like the air he breathes. If you breathe a different air from mine, you are already living on another planet and have already fallen a victim to the terrible spell of that stanza of my poem "On the Rhine." I cannot even think this thought without trembling to the very depths of my being. [The reference is to the next to the last stanza of the poem: "As if your light so far away shone into my darkness from some remote star which snatched you from me forever."]

Kierling, May 21, 1839

—My life is a quiet listening, brooding and longing and an uninterrupted soul-searching. I have thrown myself completely into nature's arms. Since yesterday the weather has been the way I like it. Warm, rainy, with thunderstorms, alternating with bright hours in which one feels the approach of the rain. The forests are full of stirring life and steam from their joyful labors. The whole valley is very much alive. Alongside the brook rich streams of life pulse audibly. I am quite ready to be caught up in the stream and carried whither it will. I need help for I am sick. The stucco is flaking off my fate in my loneliness; I look into all the cracks and crannies, and when the cracks open, they open wide. When unhappiness is the king of one's life, one had better recognize its sovereignty at once, otherwise it comes and makes the rebel feel its power in tenfold intensity at its chosen hour. I am going back to the old magicians for relief, I mean, the spirits of nature. I am again sinking into a demonic state of mind. The steaming valley deadened my pain today as beneficently as a magic cauldron in which herbs are brewing which make one invisible, etc.

Vienna, June 30, 1839

—Who has genius? Can a woman possess it? Foolish question. The man and woman possess it together. I only worked with half my soul as long as I was unloved, and when I am separated from you, that is the way it is. . . .

Stuttgart, February 26, 1840

I could not resist dear Emilie's plea that I stay here if I did not think of you and the joy of seeing you again. The atmosphere of marked respect in which I live here has a cheering and inspiring quality, but the separation from you makes me a wretched and partial creature. Yesterday I played some of our Ischl songs on the violin and thought of you with ardent longing as I played. My poem *Die Albigenser* which, I often think, may separate me from you forever, has for that reason become repulsive to me and I can work at it only with the greatest distaste. Nothing worth while, therefore, will ever come of this poem. I shall never be able to complete it successfully.

Weinsperg, June 30, 1840

—This afternoon I sat on Kerner's tower and looked across at the forest-covered mountain. Then I remembered the forests which I have seen with you; and the one I was looking at seemed so forsaken and sad and my whole life without you so depressing that I should gladly have flung it all to the winds. What do I have, what am I, if you are not mine? All is nothing without you. My inmost being is a realm of death.

Ischl, July 29, 1840

You have a place in my heart that nothing, absolutely nothing else, can fill. I have to let the days pass me by without you, and they lack a soul. They are just shadows which make believe they have life. Ischl, rich in a thousand memories, contains nothing but them to touch my heart. Even lovely nature can awake only half my feelings, since you are not here. Oh, my dearest, my only one, if you were only here for a single kiss! In order to get any work done I have to try continually to key down my thoughts of you, and my work is so necessary. If only I were well enough off to devote myself in complete leisure to my unhappiness. Yet such thoughts are not right; I should praise my situation for not allowing me the leisure to think through fully how completely I have missed and lost all the things in this life which might have availed me. Do you know, I am delighted that the number of my gray hairs is increasing!

Vienna, October 5, 1840

—I must call your attention to a contradiction in you which hurts me. You assert that you can no longer believe in me and can imagine my heart growing cold and forsaking you; and yet you often permit yourself to treat me in a way which can only be inspired in you by a very strong feeling of assurance in its most high-spirited and intense form. What a contradiction! In the moments when your love for me is suppressed because of some supposed shortcoming on my part, your distorted conception of my character is revealed, and you act toward me as one acts when one's words and acts are no longer under the surveillance of a loving respect. I shall show you that I have a control over my all too violent emotions which you shall respect. Good night.

Stuttgart, May 8, 1841

Thank God, another day over! The best thing about these days is that their passing brings me nearer to you. Thus a passion makes us rich and poor. I cannot enjoy anything without you, or rather, I only truly enjoy you. But when I hold you against my heart I regret the passing of every instant, as one regrets the passing forever of a beautiful human life. Listen, Sophie, evenings when I am writing you I have attacks of a fever of longing, and I talk aloud to you in my bed. I am going to have a bad time of it waiting such a long time before I am with you again.

Stuttgart, May 12, 1841 (afternoon)

We are one. Nothing must separate us. Nothing. It would be better to die and cease to exist entirely, wouldn't it?

Our love has grown greater and more serious. It is no longer in me, I am in it. It is my god. God's strong hand presses me so firmly to you that I can only sigh and struggle with the overwhelming bliss; my soul no longer has any breath unless it can draw breath from your kisses. Ah, Sophie, dear Sophie!

Stuttgart, May 16, 1841

Oh, I am so sick of people this evening. I shall have to be impolite in order to have some peace. They drive me to an acme of depression. They all have nothing to say to each other or to me, and yet they keep visiting me and torturing me. Oh, only a draught, a life-giving drop of your dear soul, and I could go on panting across the desert. Who knows who is sitting by the spring I have so long been deprived of, alas, at the spring of my life and of my heart's youth? Who knows what good-for-nothing is sitting by it and, taking no joy in it, calmly drinking a glass of beer? I even begrudge you your circle of friends. Today is Sunday; who knows whom you sat with at table in the café! Alas!

Vienna, February 12, 1842

If my love for you is mortal, as you seem to think, then everything about me is mortal; if your love were not the highest and dearest of my possessions, it could only be because I were dead. Do not doubt; my heart is as alive for you as ever it was, even though in all other respects I feel in it a sad dying away. My last green belongs to you, though all else withers and vanishes. You think the spark has gone out because so many ashes bury it. My being is becoming ever quieter and more withdrawn, but it takes you with it into its most secret loneliness. You are with me always and everywhere. Do not lose faith in me.

Vienna, March [?], *1842*

I dreamed tonight that I said to you: "What a pity about that hour yesterday; it might have been a very happy one." It was really a very happy one for me, because for the first time in a long while I again saw that heavenly light of a great love shining in your eyes. In your usual moods the light rarely shows because it is darkened by doubts. But yesterday your heart beat through all the doubts, and I was very happy. Oh, dear Sophie, dearest heart.

Vienna, August 17, 1842

All night long the joy of yesterday continued to stir my heart, which refused to go to sleep, weary as the rest of me was. Only when I am with you do I belong to life; separated from you, I can no longer draw a genuine and fresh breath. Sweetheart! When I am with you, there is still, in spite of my age, springtime in my veins and I have a voluptuous yearning to die in your arms.

Unterdöbling, August [?], *1843*

I promised you to write again today; you would have done better not to say good night so coldly and curtly, for then you would have received some of my lovely forest thoughts which are so filled with you. Instead I say briefly, but not coldly, "Good night, dear heart."